WHAT OTHERS ARE SAYING

Nothing can strike more fear and loathing into the hearts of an HR professional than the words, "workplace investigation". In her book, Diane demystifies this challenging, complex and litigious process by providing clear, concise and actionable steps. A valuable how-to handbook for any HR professional navigating the workplace investigation for the first time or the fiftieth!

—Mary Nummelin
VP of People and Organizational Best Practice
Polar Electro Inc.

This is the ultimate Guide to workplace investigations. Diane Pfadenhauer's book is a needed tool for every Human Resource professional and Labor and Employment lawyer. This book should not be "tucked away" in a library but should be used on a very regular basis.

—Glenn J. Franklin, Esq.
Partner
Franklin, Gringer & Cohen

Diane Pfadenhauer's *Workplace Investigations: Discrimination and Harassment* is a comprehensive and handy reference tool for Human Resources professionals and attorneys alike. This "user-friendly" guide lays out in a very digestible and organized fashion everything you need to know about conducting investigations, along with incisive comments and practical tips. The book is easy to use as a reference tool for the experienced investigator, as well as an introduction for the novice whose task it is to investigate very sensitive issues. To conduct a proper investigation, planning is the key; with Diane's book, you will be totally prepared. I highly recommend this valuable resource to all of my colleagues.

—Jules Halpern, Esq.
Principal
Halpern Employment Law Advisors

This book explicitly details every element of a workplace investigation. The insights into the fine points of the investigation are enumerated in such a fundamental way. Using this as a guideline will transform any investigation into a series of defined and logical steps leading to a thorough exploration and well determined outcome. Excellent tool!

—Barbara Gebhardt
President
Opus Staffing

Diane provides business owners and HR professionals with a clearly written, road map of how to proceed in conducting a Workplace Investigation of employee misconduct. Diane's approach is methodical and instinctive, peppered with real life scenarios you will encounter making the reading real and the process manageable. This book is a must in every manager's library.

Jeanne Stewart, SPHR
President, Human Resources Association of New York
President, HR on the Move, LLC.

EMPLOYMENT PRACTICES SERIES

WORKPLACE INVESTIGATIONS

Discrimination and Harassment

EMPLOYMENT PRACTICES SERIES

WORKPLACE INVESTIGATIONS

Discrimination and Harassment

Diane M. Pfadenhauer, SPHR, Esq.

DataMotion Publishing
New York

Datamotion Publishing, LLC
1019 Fort Salonga Road, Suite 10-333
Northport, NY 11768-2209
www.datamotionpublishing.com

CONTENTS

About the Author

Diane M. Pfadenhauer, SPHR, Esq.

With over twenty years of experience in human resources and as an attorney, Diane is president of Employment Practices Advisors, Inc., a boutique firm specializing in litigation consulting (including workplace investigations and expert witness testimony on human resource practices) and human resource consulting encompassing a broad spectrum of tactical and strategic human resource practices and compliance, including interim staff, risk prevention and developing human resource strategies to support business goals and objectives. She is also a professor in the M.B.A. program at St. Joseph's College in New York. Prior to her position at St. Joseph's, Ms. Pfadenhauer spent over a decade as an adjunct professor in graduate programs throughout the New York metropolitan area.

An active member in community and professional organizations, Diane is admitted to New York State Bar. She is a frequent speaker and writer and her articles have appeared in industry publications including *HR Magazine, HR Advisor, The Journal of Private Equity, Law Technology News, the Journal of Corporate Renewal,* and periodicals published by Dow Jones, Inc., and the New York Bar Association. She has conducted numerous continuing legal education programs for various bar associations throughout the country on the subjects of employment practices and workplace investigations and is considered an expert on the subject of workplace investigations. She is certified as a Senior Professional in Human Resources (SPHR) by the Human Resources Certification Institute. Diane is also the writer and editor of the award-winning *StrategicHRLawyer* weblog *(www.strategichrlawyer. com),* read by over 25,000 unique visitors per month from over fifty countries. She was recently awarded the *New York State Liberty Award* for her pro bono work in Louisiana following the devastation of Hurricane Katrina.

Diane received her law degree, *cum laude,* from St. John's University School of Law, where she was awarded the ABA/BNA Award for Excellence in the Study of Labor and Employment Law. She is a graduate of New York Institute of Technology's Center for Labor and Industrial Relations, where she received her M.S., with distinction. She received her B.A. from S.U.N.Y. Potsdam, majoring in Industrial Labor Relations.

WARNING AND DISCLAIMER

While this book strives to provide the reader with practical guidance and to provide general education on the topic at hand, it is not a substitute for adequate legal or other professional advice. The opinions within represent the opinions of the authors and editors only and therefore should not be construed as a position on the part of any particular organization or entity.

Further, nothing herein should be construed as the rendering of legal or other professional advice, and the reader is advised to consult with appropriate counsel for obtaining any advice. Reading this publication creates no attorney-client relationship between the reader and either the author or publisher.

A Note from the Author

I magine you are passing through the break room on a typical day at your office. You might expect to overhear the typical groaning about office politics, a heated debate about fund allocations or IT problems, or even a lively chat about last night's episode of the latest television craze. But what if the conversation you pick up has nothing to do with printer toner or upcoming deadlines and everything to do with an inappropriate encounter between two employees? What if, instead of the usual office atmosphere, you sense an overwhelming level of tension, fear, and hostility throughout the office?

And what if investigating the alleged misconduct is *your* responsibility?

All too often allegations of misconduct in the workplace begin with easily resolved issues such as a personality conflict, a perceived lack of respect, a feeling that a problem was not addressed seriously enough, or miscommunication. But regardless of how the situation begins, investigations of misconduct in the workplace, particularly of a sexual nature, are often highly emotionally charged. They cause a tremendous disruption in the workplace and present significant risks for all parties concerned. To add to the difficulty, there are often very few, if any, witnesses.

Workplace investigations are more prevalent these days due to the emergence of an inherently litigious society. Human resource staff members are not just responsible for monitoring and mediating misconduct issues. There are several other types of investigations that may also occur within a company. Safety, workers' compensation, investigations in unionized environments under the Fair Labor Standards Act, pre-employment, fraud, and discipline investigations are all serious concerns for most business administrators.

Part of my practice includes conducting workplace investigations in instances of allegations of employee misconduct. I have seen firsthand how quickly a small problem can escalate into a full-blown investigation, many times because the situation was not handled appropriately at the outset. Typically, the investigations I conduct are directly concerned with the employer's policies and sometimes, more specifically, with the employer's sexual harassment or discrimination policy. After twenty-plus years of experience in corporate human resources and as in-house labor and employment counsel, I have developed some very strong opinions, developed a variety of techniques, and can offer some very valuable advice on this subject. Surprisingly, I have found that human resource professionals are at times accused, and sadly sometimes rightfully so, of directing investigations poorly or being ill-equipped to conduct an adequate investigation. Moreover, in my travels in the attorney continuing legal education (CLE) circuit, I've found that attorneys can be equally ill-equipped.

In my quest to make our industry the leader in investigational standards and my little corner of the world a better place, I've decided to share what I have learned. Drawing from my extensive professional experience, I was able to develop a set of guidelines for workplace investigations and share that information with human resource professionals, business leaders and attorneys around the country. In this book I will share my approach by laying out easy-to-follow steps and explicit guidelines for workplace investigations into employee misconduct. This book is intended to be tactical, and my hope is that you, the reader, will find this information accessible and helpful, as so many other industry professionals have.

1

Retaining and Working with Outside Counsel

Let's start at the very beginning. Long before a workplace problem rears its ugly head, it is important to have a variety of systems and foundations in place. These serve the purpose of directing how the organization will address and respond to workplace issues. We begin that process, from the very beginning, with how to go about selecting an attorney to work with.

Choosing outside counsel is an important decision for any organization. The selection process should be approached systematically and as carefully as possible.

Counsel is too often selected for the wrong reasons. Sometimes, an internal employee may have a relationship with an outside firm. Or the company's outside firm may choose counsel. Worse yet, the organization may be pressed for time and need immediate action. In that case, administrators may forego the standard counsel evaluation and haphazardly choose counsel who may not be the appropriate choice for the case.

Human resource practitioners and other internal management staff need a handbook for retaining and working with outside labor and employment counsel. They need guidance to help them focus on determining the right fit for their company. This chapter is that guide.

Every company and law firm is unique. When choosing outside counsel, that fact must be considered, as the two must work well together. Employee issues are naturally delicate subjects, and the organization is responsible for choosing appropriate counsel for the case and developing a relationship with that counsel. Besides the inherent internal factors, a variety of external elements must also be considered.

Assess the Organization

Step 1 is to size up the company. Very basic elements will help to guide your selection decisions. Consider the size and location(s) of the company and proximity of the employees. What states are they located in? Are they unionized? What regulatory standards apply to the specific industry the organization is in? Also consider whether the company is privately or publicly owned. This may influence the level of complexity of operating systems and the regulatory environment affecting the organization. The human resource professional will use this information, and more, to figure out exactly what the organization needs and the type of counsel that can meet those needs.

The unique cultural environment of an organization is also very relevant. The human resource professional must review how authority is delegated within the organization and how employees in leadership positions conduct themselves. Who handles personnel issues? Are they centralized or decentralized in terms of management structure and decision-making? How are such situations approached? Does the organization "shoot first" and ask later, or (hopefully) the other way around? Are policies communicated effectively? What are the tone, spirit, and tenor of employee communication? What are the policies concerning misconduct and penalties? Are they specific or do they leave a great deal of leverage for management discretion and judgment? Does the company have any core values that may be relevant to a misconduct case? And perhaps most important, is there a trusting relationship between employees and management? Are employees satisfied with management behavior and administration of policies?

Understanding the culture of an organization is critical when choosing outside counsel. For example, pairing an organization that prides itself on fostering a nurturing, paternalistic environment with a cutthroat firm of go-getter lawyers would be disastrous.

External counsel can and should complement the role of the internal counsel or human resource professional. And, one of the first questions to ask is who will be foremost in that relationship with outside counsel. For a partnership to be successful, the roles must be clearly defined. In some companies, the human resource department serves as an advocate for employees. Others rely on the human resource department as an administrative branch or arm of management. Do employees consider the staff allies or managers? Is the human resource staff appropriately trained to handle disputes? Or do they serve as general mediators? Is it the job of inside counsel to "deal with the lawyers," or is this responsibility shared when it comes to human resource matters?

Finally, the availability of resources should also be considered. Resources can refer to funds, time, and internal expertise that could support or replace the work being done by an outside firm. An organization may have a limited budget for litigation or outside advice and counsel but still have a considerable need for counsel involvement. A new business may benefit financially from the use of a small law firm with lower hourly fees but may find that a small firm is unable to keep up with the company's growth and growing complexity. The goal is to come up with a plan that effectively confronts every issue in advance rather than reacting to a problem as it arises and haphazardly responding to it. That may mean being flexible and investing up front in counsel that can grow with the company.

The Function of Outside Counsel

People generally assume that a lawyer's job is to give advice. But counseling includes a lot more than generic guidance. A good lawyer will analyze the situation and carefully evaluate every possible option, ultimately recommending a path that will have the best result for the client.

Counseling is about problem-solving. Counselors don't give advice about how to make a problem disappear; they help clients fix the problem and prevent recurrence. To effectively counsel, a good lawyer will consider all internal and external factors before making a recommendation. Certainly, an understanding of the organization and its industry can be helpful.

Typically, a litigator knows his or her role well. But when outside counsel is involved, that role must be modified to ensure a successful collaboration. Will the organization be using outside counsel solely for litigation? Will it be relying upon it for advice and counsel? Step-by-step guidance? Decisions will have to be made concerning who will handle each part of the investigation—outside counsel, internal management, the human resource staff, or internal counsel (if available). Who will take care of union negotiations? Who will attend the depositions? Who will attend the trial? Who will handle interviews and collection of witness accounts and documentation? The success of the case is determined by the willingness of internal and external participants to cooperate and delegate appropriately. Obviously, the organization whose management thinks through these issues and puts together a plan long before the storm will be much better able to respond in the heat of the moment.

The lawyer is also responsible for providing reliable legal advice. Whether provided formally or not, legal advice educates the management team and gives them the necessary tools to handle conflicts as they arise. Most lawyers working with or for a company should dispense this kind of advice in accessible, common language that lay persons can under-stand and apply.

Besides giving guidance and taking on a share of the investigation, external counsel can be an ally to the human resource department. For example, the internal political climate may motivate internal staff to ask the outside counsel to deliver bad news to management.

Last, outside counsel is considered to be a trusted business advisor and, as such, should have a solid understanding of the industry and the individual organization. Failing to understand how an organization is unique hinders counsel's ability to provide more than generic legal advice. Counsel should do some homework, allowing for tailored business and legal advice.

Assessing Inside Experts

Before dividing up responsibilities, the knowledge and skill of in-house counsel, internal management, and human resource professionals should be evaluated. The worst-case scenario is assigning employees tasks for which they are grossly unprepared. For example, if an internal general counsel is asked to comply with a law he or she has never heard of, the process will be delayed so the staff member can be educated. The same goes for external counsel. An outside lawyer cannot serve effectively unless he or she is aware of laws and standards specific to the industry or the subject matter at hand.

The training skills required of human resource professional runs the gamut. Every company requires and expects different levels of ability. Some assume internal staff members can handle investigations. Other companies expect less independence and more general support from human resource professionals. Regardless of training or experience, internal counsel must be prepared to coordinate his or her activities with the outside attorney. Less experienced human resource professionals will need tremendous support when working on the analysis and materials preparation. Naturally, this will cost the company a little more. Experienced investigators will need minimal guidance but should still be willing to cooperate and delegate.

Obviously, organizations would benefit significantly from employing a competent staff that understands basic employment law and can collaborate well with counsel. Experts aren't always necessary, but employees should have the ability to self-evaluate and ask for clarification when needed.

Even the best staff will suffer under a strict time constraint. Sometimes there are simply not enough hands to get the job done, no matter how competent those hands may be. Establishing realistic objectives is essential for success. Otherwise, investigators will have to cut corners to meet deadlines. A rushed investigation may appear to be sufficient and accurate at first, but eventually those seams will start to show. Holes in the case will eventually become apparent, and the investigation could be called into question. When the workload is potentially too much, enlisting the help of the outside attorney or other expert may be the best option.

The internal human resource professional must also be prepared to handle internal conflicts. The truth is human resource staff members are not always the appropriate choice for internal investigations. For example, no employee should investigate the conduct of a superior or a colleague with whom he or she is required to work closely. Objectivity is a priority, and to ignore the presence of an internal conflict jeopardizes the entire investigation. In such cases, external counsel is required.

Choosing External Counsel

The first step is to assess the expertise of the firm being considered. Is the case industry-specific? Will the lawyers working on the investigation need to understand the basic elements of a particular field? Should the firm have an understanding of that industry or laws across multiple states or countries? Comprehensive institutional knowledge means the firm does not have to conduct extensive research, which can save the client a great deal of money. But while large labor and employment firms may have the industry expertise, they sometimes lack the ability to provide support to the internal staff. An ideal choice is an industry-trained firm with experience collaborating with and guiding the internal human resource staff.

Small firms are often chosen because they can be flexible and typically cost less. But small firms usually use only local attorneys, even for out-of-state cases. For obvious reasons, this is not always a good option. Knowing that this is a possibility, internal staff must ask certain questions before selecting a small firm. Will the out-of-state counsel meet all of the criteria established in the initial selection process? Will the firm comply with such requirements as investigation style, tactics, knowledge of the company, and business and industry expertise?

Every firm is different, and so are the attorneys working for that firm. Every attorney will approach his or her work with a specific objective in mind, and the company staff must be prepared to be flexible. The attorney serves as a partner in the investigation, but he or she may also take on the role of quasisupervisor. Will the associate be an occasional advisor or consistent collaborator?

Working with a team of outside attorneys can also pose some problems. In one case, the human resource staff would call the law firm and speak with whomever was available. This method proved ineffective when, during an important sensitive sexual harassment investigation, the human resource staff had to constantly re-explain details to the senior attorney on the case. Playing catch-up caused a massive delay, and important details were overlooked. This isn't to suggest that an outside team is ineffective, but clear protocols must be agreed upon for this kind of investigation to run smoothly.

How will information be communicated—formal memos, e-mails, or telephone calls? The method used must be consistent for all parties in order for them to be kept up to speed. Is the client willing to work with various attorneys, or does he or she expect to deal with the same counselor every time? Will counsel be onsite or in a separate location? While many firms will suggest that they can "do it all" to the client's specifications, their individual styles will inherently affect the flow of the investigation. Ideally, the firm's methods should complement the organization's preferred approach.

To be formally considered, firms should submit documentation detailing fee structures, examples of their work, and internal policies. They must also state whether or not they will review the company's handbooks and policy manuals at the outset, and if a fee is charged for such preliminary work. A firm that is serious about being considered will gladly take the time to get to know the organization at no charge.

Concerning Insurance

Lawsuits are more popular than ever, so many employers have invested in employment practices liability insurance (EPLI). Typically, the carrier of an EPLI policy reserves counsel selection rights. Carriers are also often allowed to agree to settlements at their own discretion. If the employer wishes not to settle a particular case, liability for the insurance company may be limited to the initial recommended amount. Loss of control is obviously a serious concern when considering the purchase of EPLI, and the issue of settlement and selection of counsel should be addressed at the purchasing stage. Risk management staff should be consulted before a decision to purchase insurance is made. In addition, the organization should be sure that its desired methods of dispute resolution are supported by the presence of insurance.

The right to choose counsel is an especially significant concern. Though it may be an expensive policy modification, a company will benefit more in the long run if it retains the right to select an employment law expert who knows the organization and industry well. A nonexpert attorney selected from the insurance carrier's panel can often cost the company more in the long run.

Regarding settlement, the employer may have no say in when or how the insurance company settles. The carrier will want to settle for the lowest amount possible, but an employer will better understand the effects of settling too early or too late. While maintaining the right to settle may cost more in terms of premiums, the employer knows his company best and can make decisions that are good for the company, not the carrier.

Division of Labor and Developing a Relationship

Certain ground rules should be established for a collaboration to be successful. Having a plan in place will ease the difficulty of the complicated work to be done later. First, the handling of fees and expenses must be addressed. If convenience is the preference, the law firm can complete the bulk of the investigation and charge the client. If the client wants to be frugal, the internal staff should take on a significant share of the work. To ensure that the company's needs are being met cost-effectively, the budget should be reviewed regularly, along with the service being provided. Communication should be open and ongoing.

Second, both parties should agree upon a lead financial contact. Will this be an individual or a team? Ensuring that the appropriate persons are responsible for bills and invoices is essential in order to eliminate conflict.

A clear division of labor is also necessary to make sure no aspect of the investigation is overlooked. Will the in-house staff serve as intermediary for the outside firm, or will the outside firm work directly with the human resource staff or management? What tasks are the internal staff members expected and qualified to do? What are external lawyers responsible for completing? Which activities can be completed on company time? Which activities can be completed on the law firm's time? And what other company responsibilities will affect the staff's ability to address their assignments?

Litigation

Every organization will someday be involved in litigation concerning employment practices. To make the case run smoothly, roles and responsibilities should be assigned prior to a case. Internal practitioners must determine how much they will be involved in the litigation. Are they expected to attend every deposition and go over details with the attorney? More involvement often means a better defense, because company insight can be a great resource for the defense.

Throughout the litigation, the attorney may request certain documents, evidence, and other relevant material. Internal staff has a responsibility to clarify exactly what the outside attorney wants and why the material is needed. Fully understanding the purpose behind the request may help the staff to shed light on the defense.

Even after the investigation, involved parties must agree on the frequency and method of communication. Litigation can often consist of a lot of hurrying and a lot of waiting. A pressing deadline may cause a frenzy of activity, and a lot of time may pass without much communication. During a quiet period, the client may assume that the attorney has dropped the ball or isn't keeping the company in the loop.

Retaining outside employment counsel requires serious internal and external analysis. A comprehensive evaluation will enable organizations and attorneys to effectively handle their employee relations issues. If everyone puts in the effort and maintains open communications, the result is a productive and long-term relationship.

2

Advocating for the
Third-Party Investigator

There are several generally accepted methods for handling workplace investigations. The most common approach involves an investigation conducted by the internal human resource department. The findings are reported to management, and management ultimately decides on a penalty, if necessary. If litigation ensues, the human resource professional is often relieved of investigational duties, the investigation is done by the law firm's attorneys, and the human resource professional becomes a witness for the defense.

There are some problems with this approach. Counsel often finds critical errors in the investigation—often after the fact. The most common mistakes involve insufficient interview procedures. The person conducting the interview confuses the facts and has no apparent system for the order or choice of interview subjects. Interview notes are generally inadequate, and often the interviewer has overlooked key witnesses. Worse yet, the investigator may not actually interview key witnesses whose statements could be an influential determinant of the outcome of the investigation.

The second approach leaves the investigation to inside or outside counsel. This is often the preferred method if there is potential for litigation or if the investigation is prompted by a subpoena or letter from an attorney representing the complainant. The preliminary investigation must always be comprehensive and accurate; and if a trial is possible, legal expertise is even more important. This scenario, however, also has some disadvantages. Details can easily be missed, because counsel can become so focused on the depositions and mitigation of damages. In addition, counsel brought in to do an investigation may be perceived as biased in favor of the employer; and because a counsel-run investigation can be expensive, the focus may turn to money rather than determining the truth.

A third option attempts to find a balance between the other two approaches. In this third option, outside counsel oversees an investigation conducted by an internal professional. As the internal professional collects testimony and evidence, counsel monitors and advises. This often back-and-forth approach is a great way to prevent mistakes and ensure an accurate investigation. Another advantage to this approach is the ability to maximize attorney-client privilege. Certain statements may be made to counsel that are protected by the attorney-client privilege. Unfortunately, however, some advocates of this method believe that attorney-client privilege can be invoked like a magical force field to shield the entire investigation from the eyes of opposing counsel. If, however, the results of the investigation are to be used in the defense of any upcoming litigation, the investigation itself becomes discoverable. A further disadvantage to this technique is that counsel must rely on third-party information provided to him or her by the internal professional conducting the investigation. All of the facts are filtered through an often inexperienced investigator, and many details are missed in transition.

In fact, inexperienced investigators are a problem regardless of the investigation method. Too many employers wrongly assume that internal professionals are qualified to conduct an investigation. In actuality, many human resource professionals, and even some attorneys, are not trained or experienced in workplace investigations. Human resource professionals are required to manage a variety of duties. They are responsible for everything ranging from benefits administration to employee relations and training. With so many other responsibilities, many are justifiably unable to become investigation experts. Besides being overwhelmed by the sheer volume of work an investigation requires, internal professionals may also be far too involved in office politics to be objective, regardless of their good intentions.

Where all of these approaches fail is in a commitment to uncovering the truth. This naturally happens because focus is divided. Attorneys focus on the defense of the claim like a well-thought-out chess match, and the human resource professional is forced to work around the internal political environment, usually taking the matter far more seriously than other internal management. An investigation in which the facts come second is a failed investigation. The defense cannot stand on an investigation that is full of holes. Employers would be better served to invest in an outside investigator early on, rather than paying top dollar for a defense attorney to clean up the mess.

Third-party investigators are becoming an increasingly popular option. Employers are often accused of conducting biased, self-serving investigations. Due to widespread discontent with common practices, regulations concerning objectivity and neutrality in business management have been established. One need only look at the regulations in the financial arena as an example.

To further reinforce the need for third-party investigators, employees also doubt the neutrality of internal investigators. Across the board, employees demand a system of checks and balances, fairness, and objectivity. For this reason, companies have looked to third-party investigators to handle internal issues.

Fair and Unbiased Investigators

Parties on the other side of an investigation will always doubt the neutrality and objectivity of the investigation. Human resource staff members are often viewed as part of management and find themselves, at times, in the difficult position of being investigator, prosecutor, and jury for every investigation. Some professionals say that serving in these three positions simultaneously is no problem, claiming they have no trouble being fair and unbiased. Even if that was an honest statement, no one involved in the case will find that claim believable.

The outside investigator will not be affected by the outcome of the case and has no preconceived opinions or suspicions. Also, a pair of fresh eyes will most likely pick up on aspects of the case that internal parties might overlook. An outside investigator is like an arbitrator, unbiased and objective.

Fairness Perceived

Unlike the human resource department, the outside investigator will not be viewed as a member of management. Employees will expect neutrality and objectivity from an unrelated investigator. Of course, any investigator hired by management will come under some scrutiny. But an effective investigator will be able to assuage doubts by portraying a necessary element of fairness that an internal investigator cannot. Also, objectivity and neutrality will be important if the investigation is challenged by plaintiff's counsel or by the Equal Employment Opportunity Commission.

Attorney-Client Privilege

Utilizing the *Ellerth/Faragher* defense, which the Supreme Court established in *Faragher v. City of Boca Raton* and *Burlington Industries v. Ellerth*, employers may avoid certain hostile work environment claims. This defense depends on early detection and prevention of harassment. A successful defense depends on the counsel's ability to demonstrate prompt and remedial action from the employer.

The use of the attorney-client privilege is not always a fallback solution. In some cases, the attorney-client privilege may be lost. If the defense counsel conducts an investigation and the reasonableness of the investigation becomes an issue in the case, the privilege is lost. Ultimately, defense counsel becomes a witness. In many cases defense attorneys may be forced to release all notes and disclose any guidance given to the client.

Some firms have responded by using only outside professionals to conduct investigations. This way, it is clear what matters are privileged as legal advice and what matters are fact-finding by the investigator. Thus, by using an outside neutral investigator, the organization is in the best position to assert the attorney-client privilege without successful challenges by opposing counsel. An internal investigator will likely be viewed as just another witness, and the investigation as required evidence along with a clear delineation in roles between lawyer, client and fact-finder.

Experienced Professionals

A professionally trained investigator will likely have more experience and expertise as a fact-finder than will an internal human resource professional or outside labor and employment attorney. An attorney or other lay professional trained in investigations has a better understanding of litigation and will likely conduct a much more thorough investigation. But in addition to legal expertise, which is often helpful, the investigator's other professional experience may affect the quality and professionalism of the investigation.

Ensuring that the investigator has comprehensive knowledge of workplace dynamics is essential for a successful investigation. The investigator should be aware of internal policies and practices within the workplace, in general, and what behaviors can take place despite those policies. He or she should also be well versed in the intricacies of office politics. A solid background in workplace essentials will help the investigator conduct an unbiased investigation.

Being Taken Seriously and Scheduling

When an outside investigator is brought in, management sends a clear message to employees that it understands the seriousness of the matter. Also, while participants may not respond seriously or honestly to questions from an internal interviewer, an outside investigator will command their respect.

Scheduling interviews is often difficult for inside investigators. So much outside of the investigation remains to be done each day. Besides the increased workload, taking employees away from their work is disruptive and causes confusion about company priorities. Internal investigators also have to deal with senior-level employees. If a senior-level employee disapproves of or doubts the investigation, he or she can purposely insert scheduling conflicts to hinder the investigation. Internal investigators may feel pressure to go along with the changes to protect their jobs. These signals of disapproval could be apparent enough to discourage key employees from participating or disclosing valuable information.

An outside investigator will take pressure off of internal staff, scheduling will be less disruptive to productivity, and employees will likely be more willing to participate.

Office Politics

One of the biggest hazards with any investigation is the potential for political conflict. When an investigation is conducted by someone in-house, multiple parties are placed in awkward positions. No matter what the findings, someone will invariably be concerned with the outcome. Inevitably, some blame will be placed on the internal investigator. Even if the investigator was truly unbiased, anyone adversely affected by the results will claim the investigator was self-serving or biased in some way.

Organizations work diligently to promote cohesiveness and cooperation. They spend an inordinate amount of time and money on programs to increase employee morale, well-being and cohesiveness. When an internal staff member is granted an unreasonable amount of power and influence, others may resent the authority and refuse to cooperate. Using an internal investigator is naturally divisive and destructive to even the most positive office environment.

Of course, retaliation is also an issue. Both the complainant and any of the witnesses could be targeted, and the human resource professional on the case must be vigilant. In many cases, the investigator can be ostracized or punished in some way by other employees. When one individual is called upon by management to judge another, employees become angry. If employees don't like the results of the investigation, the investigator is considered incompetent, selfish, or manipulative. If an outside investigator is responsible for the factual conclusions, internal staff members are spared the blame.

Any time an internal employee conducts an investigation, he or she must deal with a variety of political, emotional, and social conflicts. An inside investigation can be a recipe for disaster or, at a minimum, subject to criticism by opposing counsel. Outside investigators, however, bring a level of professionalism, expertise, neutrality, and objectivity to the investigation.

Ability to Get the Organization Back on Track

The aftermath of an investigation must also be handled delicately. Investigations can be stressful and drawn out, and if conducted by an internal investigator, they can feel like a witch hunt. The goal is to get back to work as quickly as possible and with as little disruption or conflict as possible. Outside investigators make this much easier for management. Rather than conducting the investigation and justifying the results, management is only responsible for making decisions relating to the factual conclusions made by the investigator. Focus can be shifted again to work, and management will not be viewed as operating under a double standard—where on the one hand it expends time, money and energy to get employees to play nicely with each other, while on the other hand it places itself in the job of seemingly conducting a witch hunt.

EEOC Guidance

In *Enforcement Guidance: Vicarious Employer Liability for Unlawful Harassment by Supervisors,* the Equal Employment Opportunity Commission established clear guidelines about workplace investigations. "Specifically, the employer should ensure that the individual who conducts the investigation will objectively gather and consider the relevant facts. The alleged harasser should not have supervisory authority over the individual who conducts the investigation and should not have any direct or indirect control over the investigation. Whoever conducts the investigation should be well-trained in the skills that are required for interviewing witnesses and evaluating credibility." The first tactic a plaintiff may employ is to attack the credibility of the investigator; therefore, compliance with these guidelines is critical. The investigator will be closely evaluated on every aspect of the investigation and his or her personal qualifications. This kind of scrutiny will occur even if the investigator works closely with highly trained defense counsel.

Conflict resolution, on any scale, is a part of every work environment. When an investigation is conducted, fairness and objectivity are paramount. If employees can see that a neutral outside investigator conducted a fair and credible investigation, they will be more accepting of the results, even if the results are unpopular. In fact, organizational research has shown that employees are typically more interested in the process (and its perception of objectivity and fairness) than the result, whether unpopular or not. And during the trial, they will be less averse to participating openly and honestly.

3

Preparing for the Storm

Truly understanding how to approach an investigation means knowing what to expect. While you may have no idea about the details of the specific incident(s) in question, you should be prepared for the first sign of trouble.

There are several ways you may be informed about the need for an investigation:

- An employee files a claim or report as required by the organization's policy.
- Management learns of a possible violation.
- You receive correspondence from attorney.
- You receive correspondence from an administrative agency.
- You overhear discussion about, or are directly informed of, possible misconduct.

The effective resolution of conflict in the workplace is often contingent upon proactive prevention programs including sound policies, effective training, and comprehensive intervention and follow up. Thus, an effective investigation begins with sound policies in place that are consistently and fairly followed. Even before you are aware of the need for an investigation, you need to carefully consider the company policies with regard to misconduct. Familiarize yourself with the general guidelines that the company has in place. This applies whether you are reviewing your policies overall or if you suddenly find yourself thrust into an investigation. When I do investigations, I typically will ask to see the employee handbook or policy manual prior to meeting with anyone in order to review some of these polices. So, what exactly are you looking for?

To assess all of the company's policies, there are seven basic questions you must ask. The results of these questions will yield a great deal about the organization's culture, method of problem-solving, consistency, communication style, and the seriousness with which the organization addresses these types of problems. The questions are:

1. Is there consistency in all policies?
2. Are the policies clear and easily understood?
3. Do the policies utilize a maximum reservation of rights?
4. Is there consistency in application for all policies?
5. Do the policies contain all of the appropriate and required elements?

6. Are positions of authority and their responsibilities clearly defined? (In other words, who is considered management, and what is the hierarchy?)
7. How do employees know about these policies?

For each specific policy, do the following:
1. Review the types of misconduct covered by the policy, the roles and responsibilities of management and employees.
2. Review the extent to which the policy has been disseminated and whether training has been done. This will determine whether all parties have been properly put on notice as to the policies' existence and their responsibilities under each of the policies.
3. Review guidelines articulated under the policies with respect to specific steps that management will take in the event of a complaint of alleged violation. Review specific steps that aggrieved employees are required to take to resolve their workplace issues.

Specific Policies to Review

When confronted with an allegation of employee misconduct, don't plunge headfirst into dealing with the problem without reviewing relevant policies. Often, the discovery is made that the employer failed to follow company policy, which can be detrimental to the defense of the case. Moreover, previously unnoticed and neglected inconsistencies are identified as glaring oversights by opposing counsel.

The following policies are relevant from two major perspectives. First, each organization should review each of these policies with the goal of providing effective resolutions and prevention of workplace misconduct. Second, these policies should also be reviewed by any investigator conducting a workplace investigation. Depending upon the facts and circumstances of the allegations, these policies may or may not be relevant.

1. EEO/Harassment Policy
   a. Review coverage, reporting process, and any mandatory steps. Were they followed?
   b. Review reporting requirements, notice issues, and any statements regarding how an investigation will be handled.
   c. Review the nonretaliation provisions, and plan how you will demonstrate that the claimant and witnesses were protected and had avenues for reporting any claims of retaliation.
   d. Determine what type of feedback you will give the claimant and accused. Plan now how you will address inconclusive findings, findings of fact, etc.
2. Discipline/Discharge
   a. An allegation of harassment can ultimately result in discipline if violation of the harassment policy has occurred. The discipline/discharge policy should be checked for consistency with the harassment policy. For example, if the discipline policy requires additional steps

or warnings that the harassment policy does
not, you must reconcile how you will handle
instances that are covered by both policies.

3. Code of Conduct

    a. Some organizations have a code of conduct
        that is used to outline general guidelines of
        appropriate behavior. These policies may or
        may not include infractions that would also
        violate the EEO/harassment policy. Therefore,
        drafters and reviewers of these policies should
        ensure that they work in concert, rather than
        contrary to each other.

4. Ethics

    a. More and more organizations have
        implemented policies on ethical conduct.
        Going beyond general guidelines of behavior,
        companies now address and prevent securities
        violations, fraud, accounting improprieties,
        security issues, and more. While the EEO/
        harassment policy is maintained by a chief
        human resource officer, ethics policies are
        typically maintained by a chief compliance
        officer. When an allegation is brought under
        either policy, the organization may find
        violations under both.

5. Privacy

    a. Employees typically have a seemingly high
        expectation of privacy in the workplace. They
        view their desks as personal space, they view

their lockers as their own, and they view their computers as devices for both business and personal communication.

b. Policies must articulate clearly the level of privacy that employees can expect at work. Moreover, employers need to behave in a way that reinforces this policy.

6. Workplace Searches

a. Related to the issue of privacy, employers must clearly state in their policies that they reserve the right to conduct searches anywhere in the workplace. Does the policy retain this right? How will the investigator handle a review of employee personal space in the workplace, computers, lockers or desks?

7. Violence

a. When an employee alleges a violation of the EEO/harassment policy, he or she may also allege that inappropriate touching or battery occurred.

b. Violence in the workplace may also be precipitated by warning signs exhibited by the employee. Opposing counsel may allege that the warning signs were obvious and that the employer was negligent in failing to heed them. Of course, immediately addressing threatening behavior can prevent not only violence, but allegations of negligence from occurring.

8. Technology
   a. Technology in the workplace has often been called the "smoking gun" of discovery. Even though they know that e-mail and other documents can be recovered even after being deleted, employees often underestimate the significance of an electronic paper trail. Investigators often find that employees' haphazard actions still demonstrate a lack of appreciation for this concept of document and correspondence retrieval.
   b. Employers need to take into account the trends in electronic discovery in the development of their technology policies, as well as the increasingly diverse methods that employees use to communicate. They need to be sure that their technology policies are broad and encompass all forms of technology used to communicate in the workplace, both on- and off-site, and both employer- and employee-owned. Employers should start by ensuring that their privacy and technology policies are coordinated. The investigator needs to know how requests for such evidence will be handled.
9. Requirement of Employees to Participate in Investigation
   a. All too often, employees refuse to participate in an investigation. Relevant policies must disclose

an employee's obligation to participate and
to turn over relevant evidence upon demand
by the investigator. The policy should also
communicate the consequences for failing to
do so. Thus, when the investigator comes upon
a reticent witness, he or she will know how to
deal with the witness in accordance with the
policy.

Internal Considerations

Assessing the company policies is a great preliminary
tool and should be repeated every time a charge or claim
is made. But with regard to a specific investigation, there
are some internal considerations you must address before
diving in:

- political factors and how these will be dealt
  with so that they do not impede or hamper the
  investigation,
- organizational factors such as an understanding of
  the organization, authority and control, etc.
- availability of internal resources—such as time
  and staff,
- internal expertise,
- centralized and decentralized environments,
- corporate culture,
- the presence of EPLI and its impact on selection of
  outside counsel and reporting obligations, and
- alternative dispute resolution policies.

In short, every organization is different. While a solid investigation strategy will work for any company, don't underestimate the importance of getting to know the nuances of your particular case.

* An important note on internal considerations: they should not influence any aspect of the investigation, but they invariably may. Be especially wary of any effect on objectivity.

Additionally, there are more specific factors to consider when working out your plan for a particular investigation. These include

- the type and scope of the investigation (misconduct, sexual harassment, etc.);
- the complexity of the issue and potential difficulty in finding a resolution;
- prognosis: the possibility of litigation and expected impact on the work environment;
- criminal or other conduct that must be reported, and if so, to which administrative agencies;
- what the claimant is seeking to obtain by bringing his or her complaint;
- what damages or injury the accuser has suffered;
- what is at risk for the claimant and accused and for other witnesses;
- work history with regard to the claimant and accused;

- relationship between the claimant and accused;
- performance record of the claimant and accused;
- all correspondence and other communication between the claimant and accused, electronic and otherwise; and
- prior complaints, performance issues, or disciplinary issues relating to all parties.

Organizational Research Findings

A great deal of research has been done in the area of conflict resolution in the workplace from both a legal perspective and from the perspective of organizational effectiveness. Each organization develops it own culture and operational norms. These influence the company's general attitude and practices concerning litigation and conflict resolution. Every organization has developed a method of handling conflicts that is a product of its management style, tolerance, and risk aversion. Like it or not, these methods may be stated or unstated, consistent or inconsistent, sophisticated or simplistic.

I've already mentioned that employees who believe a system is fair are less likely to pursue outside action and more likely to be productive. Effective investigations and conflict resolutions ensure that disputes are less likely to be disruptive.

While lawyers often tend to focus on risk avoidance and minimization, organizational experts focus on the disruptive nature of workplace conflicts and how they can be ameliorated to quickly get the organization back on track. Organizational researchers have successfully identified the characteristics that, aside from the legal parameters that are required, differentiate an adequate program from an effective program. In other words, while a program may meet minimal legal standards, policies may not be ones that promote employee trust and participation.

Organizational experts recommend reviewing the following factors for effective conflict resolutions and workplace investigations:

1. Availability of expert resources
   a. Are there appropriately trained individuals in the workplace to receive and handle employee complaints?
2. Preconditions for internal investigators
   a. Are the internal individuals who are asked to conduct investigations properly trained?
   b. Are internal investigators free from bias or preconceived notions of guilt or innocence?
   c. Are internal investigators free from organizational political pressures?
3. Level of employee contribution
   a. Do employees have the opportunity to be heard?
   b. Will witnesses be interviewed if suggested by the claimant or accused?
4. Investigator impartiality and independence
   a. Will one party or department (such as the human resource department) serve as the role of fact finder, judge and jury?
   b. Is the investigator merely an arm of the legal department or senior management?

5. Timeliness and speed of the process
   a. Is the problem perceived as being swept under the rug?
6. Consistency with which complaints are resolved
   a. Are some complaints handled aggressively, while others are barely investigated?
7. Management support
   a. Does management accept the findings and recommendations of the investigator and take remedial measures when suggested?
8. Consistency of process and the organizational culture
   a. Does an autocratic organization have a system too inconsistent with its leadership style to be believed?

Researchers have determined that employees respond very well to a clear, consistent investigational policy. They tend to look beyond who won or lost, focusing instead on the process and provided explanation. Even if employees have no information about the accused's guilt or innocence, they will lean on the reliability of the investigational system when assessing fairness. More importantly, the type of process followed is less important to employees than how efficiently investigators implement the steps.

4

The Twelve-Step Investigation Process

Y ou've gotten to this section of the book as a result of one or two scenarios. First, you are either methodically following the guidelines in the book to ensure the organization is best prepared in the event an investigation becomes necessary; or second, you are in the heat of the moment and need to do an investigation NOW! The following steps are not intended to be a rigid process for conducting a workplace investigation. Remember that every investigation is unique. The goal is to provide guidance for common issues and a framework around which you can develop your own strategies.

1. Intake of Information

The initial complaint need not be in writing for you to take notice. An understanding of the basics of employment law tells us that the obligation to look into the matter further need not be precipitated by a formal written complaint. If your practice is to request a formal written complaint, you can certainly ask a complainant to prepare one for you; however, your obligations are not alleviated if he or she fails to or refuses to do so. Your response to the complainant should indicate that you take the claim very seriously. Above all, do not suggest that the claim is not legitimate or threaten retaliation.

Assuming that you are on the receiving end of a complaint by an employee, understand what your obligations under the employer's policy. For example, if you are a manager and are required to contact the human resource department as soon as possible, then be sure to do so. You will also want to assure the complainant that the complaint will be taken seriously and that you need to forward the information on to the appropriate parties in the organization. You cannot assure him or her of complete confidentiality, as some information will be shared should there be an investigation. However, you can advise the complainant that you take the complaint seriously and that you will only share information with those with whom you are required to under the policy.

At this point a decision will need to be made about the employee's next steps. Give appropriate directions, in accordance with the proper parties in the workplace (i.e. the human resource department), regarding whether or not he or she should return to work or take some time off. Do not use this time to delve into the details of the complaint just yet; obtain enough information to have a general understanding of what is going on. This may include some cursory written materials the complainant has, some initial documentation, or the like. Then, end your discussion and tell the complainant that someone will get back to him or her.

At this point you should be sure that the appropriate internal parties are aware of the situation. Each organization will have a certain protocol to be established. Be sure you know what that is so that you can minimize any delays.

Take deep breath, and go on to the next step.

2. Outline Your Plan

Once you fully understand the essence of the complaint and assuming that you are the one doing the investigation, you will need to start devising a detailed plan of attack. First, identify which policies will dictate your procedures and what issues or concerns are raised. Go back to Chapter 3 to gain an understanding of the types of policies that influence workplace investigations. Even if you fully understand the organization's policies, it is a good idea to go back and review them, as I doubt that you've read them in a while.

Second, decide who is ultimately in charge of the investigation. This may be something you learn while reviewing company policies. Possibilities include members of senior management or human resources and inside or outside attorneys.

If you are responsible for the investigation, you will have to make an executive decision about whom to notify about the investigation and when they should be alerted of the situation. Keep in mind there may be multiple tiers of management, including divisional and departmental supervisors. Disclosure should be considered on a need-to-know basis.

One of the most important details you must know about doing an investigation at the outset is to have a solid understanding of what you are ultimately being asked to do. You may be asked to gather the facts and present them to another party (i.e., senior management). You may be asked to gather facts and make a determination as to whether there has been a violation of company policy. You may also be asked for recommendations as to how to handle the parties at the end of the investigation. Still further, you may be asked, if you are a lawyer, to provide a legal conclusion as to whether the alleged activity constitutes harassment or discrimination. This will help guide you when you present your findings to the appropriate parties. However, your primary goal is to gather the facts as fairly, accurately, expediently and objectively as possible.

After looking at the relevant policies, review any pertinent files and any documents and other evidence the complainant initially provided. Initially, there may not be much—perhaps just a letter from an attorney, a detailed complaint from the victim or a formal complaint from a regulatory agency. But the evidence you have so far may provide leads for other information.

Begin making several lists. Make a list of people to interview. Include the claimant, the accused, any possible witnesses, and any employees or outside individuals who may be able to provide insight about work history, previous incidents and behavioral history, and the relationship between the accuser and accused. Keep this list in your investigation file, and for each person on the list, briefly outline what you need to find out from him or her. This list will continually be adjusted as you go through your interviews and as new information is gathered. Then, as you prepare for each interview, you will have an overview of what you need to find out from each person.

Your next list should be a list of evidence you believe you need. Your interviewees will likely reference policies, procedures, e-mail correspondence, conversations, etc. Obtain copies of these in order to verify their existence. You will want to confirm that your interviewees have seen some of the evidence, if others so allege. In other words, let's say that in a particular department there is a procedure for scheduling time off and that scheduling time off is relevant to your investigation. You will want to know what the procedure is, where it can be found, how it was communicated to employees, and whether certain employees actually received the policy.

Find out if law enforcement is currently or could possibly be involved. If the police are already working on the case, then the case encompasses much more than office misconduct. In addition, determine what regulatory agencies must be notified, if any. For example, in some health care environments, allegations that infer omissions in the care of patients may have to be reported to certain authorities. The presence of outside authorities may influence your investigation from the standpoint that these outside regulators may be required to do their own investigation. You will want to be sure that your activities are permitted.

Immediately make a decision about how to approach and handle both the claimant and the accused. There is no clear-cut answer here. You will have to weigh a variety of factors based upon the preliminary facts you now know. Some of the factors to weigh include:

- The seriousness of the alleged offense. Is there an accusation of battery or inappropriate touching? Is the accusation a combination of ongoing and escalating harm? Is it possibly the result of only hurt feelings? Is the accused a coworker, third party, or higher-up in the chain of command?

- The potential disruption to the workplace. What will be the impact of the removal of the accused and the accuser from the workplace?

- The possibility of further harm. Will permitting the accused to remain in the workplace while the investigation is ongoing result in the potential for further harm to the accused or others?

- The possibility of termination. If the allegations are true, will the accused be terminated? If so, the situation may be serious enough to justify removing the accused from the workplace.

- The possibility of retaliation. Will the accused or accuser be able to influence others through intimidation or otherwise during the investigation?

- What does the company's collective bargaining agreement say? If a union is present, the organization may have to consult with union leadership on the removal of someone from the workplace.

- And a final factor that is often overlooked: does the complexity and seriousness of the situation require a monitor for the workplace?

Last, and certainly not least, consider how much of the allegations should be revealed to the accused at this point. Should you share any specific details alleged, or should you wait until you formally interview the accused? Often, organizations will meet briefly with the accused to tell him or her that there has been an accusation, to explain whether or not he or she will be removed from the workplace for the duration of the investigation, and to provide a high-level overview of the nature of the complaint.

In your brief meeting with the accused, you will also want to mention a few other things. First, that the complaints are taken seriously, that the accused should treat the matter as confidential, and that he or she should not discuss the matter with other employees (without violating his or her union rights). In addition, remind the accused of the relevant employer's policies, particularly with regard to retaliation, and request that the accused not speak with or reach out to the accuser. Send the accused on his or her way, either back to work or on administrative leave, and advise the person that someone will get back to him or her.

3. Prepare for Interviews

Take a look at your list of potential interviewees and consider the order in which you will meet with them. Factor in the logistics of actually scheduling the interviews. In an ideal world, interviewees are available at the time and order you wish to speak with them. Sadly, this is almost never the case. You may find that a particular witness will be out of the office on vacation on the date you are prepared to conduct the interview. A potentially serious problem with a customer can delay an interview. As a result of these and other often unplanned events, you may not be able to interview everyone in the perfect order. In addition, some of the evidence you have requested may not be available to review with some of the witnesses.

Your first meeting will likely be a very long, detailed meeting with the accuser to gather all of the facts being alleged. When scheduling the interview, allow for ample time (possibly hours) to gather the information. Ask the person to bring in any evidence he or she may have to support the claims. This may range from a few inappropriate e-mails to a voluminous pile of documents. You will have to decide later which is relevant. At this point in your investigation you may also want to prepare a preliminary timeline of events. You will refer to this timeline often if there are a series of accusations. It will help you to gain a perspective from each witness later on as to the course of events and allegations.

Your second interview may not always be with the accused. Depending upon what the claimant told you, you may feel that you wish to corroborate some of the allegations with other witnesses before meeting with the accused. You may wish to present certain evidence to other witnesses to confirm its authenticity.

Thereafter, you will methodically go through your witnesses in the most logical order possible. Due to unavailability, time constraints or otherwise, your order may not be perfect. But you will always want to be prepared to explain why you asked the questions you asked, did the things you did, and interviewed the witnesses in the order that you did.

Choose appropriate times and private locations, bearing in mind the availability of witnesses, opposing counsel, an investigational supervisor, a shop steward, or any other individual who must be present for the meetings. Go back to the list on page 42 and consider some of these issues to decide whether you feel it is appropriate to conduct interviews on or off site. Logistically it may be easier to conduct interviews where the witnesses are, but you may feel that there would be too much disruption in the workplace to conduct them there. Be sure to bring plenty of tissues, make sure the environment is conducive to a lengthy conversation, and make sure water or other refreshments are available. Be sure to schedule in time for a break. More often than not, you will find yourself taking much more time than anticipated, and an occasional break will serve you and the interviewee well.

Be informed about cultural differences with regard to personal space, appropriate eye contact, voice inflection when asking questions, and the significance, if any, of body language during a conversation. Also be sensitive to cultural gender relations. For example, in some cultures, a one-on-one interview between a male and a female may be inappropriate, particularly when sexual misconduct is the topic.

Some cultures, for example, do not approve of female authority figures, and so male employees may refuse to answer pointed questions from a female interviewer. In that case, you may have to make adjustments. This is rare, but still worth considering.

Plan what you will address in each interview. There will be statements that you will make or questions you will pose to everyone, and there will be specifics that you address with individual witnesses. For each interview, you should address the following:

> the issue of confidentiality—that the information shared in the investigation and the interview are confidential and should not be discussed with others;
>
> why you are conducting the interview;
>
> that you are conducting a fact-finding investigation;
>
> encouraging the witness to tell the truth and to provide you with any information that may help you to find the truth;
>
> a restatement of the organization's relevant policies—such as the requirement to participate in the investigation and a restatement of the organization's harassment and nonretaliation policies;
>
> closing each interview by thanking the interviewee for participating;
>
> providing your contact information, and indicate that you welcome additional information from the witness if it comes to mind after the interview;

asking the witness if there are other witnesses who
should be spoken to;

asking the witness if there is other evidence that he or
she is aware of that can be provided to you; and

mentioning that you may wish to speak with the
witness again should you need to ask further
questions.

Beyond these general points you will want a bullet list
for each interviewee of all of the items you will address with
him or her. Again, this list is a work in progress and will be
modified as you go through your interviews.

Having your interview list, your timeline, and your list
of documentary evidence that you have or will ask for will
allow you to begin conducting your interviews.

4. Conducting Interviews

Avoid giving too much advance notice to witnesses.
Early warning allows them time to collaborate on their
responses. Interview each individual separately and in a
private room.

If there is to be more than one interviewer in the room,
plot a seating arrangement that will make the interviewee
comfortable. Speaking of comfort, don't forget to include
the basic necessities I mentioned before, such as tissues and
water. The goal is to establish a comfortable but serious environment so that the subject doesn't feel interrogated.

Always take your own notes, but also consider whether
or not to use a stenographer or objective note-taker. In an

ideal world, recording the interviews with a tape recording device and creating transcripts is an excellent supplement to your notes. However, the presence of a note-taker or recording equipment are likely to discourage participation of any witness. Again, you are best served creating an environment that encourages participation rather than one that creates an atmosphere in which a witness may be reluctant to participate openly.

Begin the interview by addressing the items you established in your interview plan in Steps 2 and 3. Review, in detail, the specific questions you developed for each of the witnesses. And do not prevent a witness from leaving, if he or she chooses to do so. If he or she simply needs a break, make sure there is no opportunity for interaction with other subjects during the interim.

The best way to handle an uncooperative witness is with gentle authority and calm. Reflect back to your understanding of why he or she may choose not to participate, and mention again the seriousness of the investigation. Restate the organization's policies with regard to participation in an interview. Give the witness the opportunity to contact you later. Remember that you are always better off encouraging the witness to cooperate with you rather than using threats or intimidation to obtain cooperation.

You may have a great list of questions and discussions to initiate with your subjects, but sometimes the hardest part is beginning. The interviewee may be nervous, and so might you. So, what do you say? First, introduce yourself, and then start with the list of details that you will address with each witness (described above). Often this is enough to break the ice so that you can move forward with the interview, putting yourself and the interviewee at ease.

Concerning the actual interview and the details you will address with each person, here are some general guidelines.

To begin with, don't forget the basic questions:

Who? What? When? Where? Why? and How?

Ask or think "so what?" for each statement made by an interviewee. Why did he or she raise this point, make this claim, etc.? What was the motive?

Also...

Avoid leading questions.

Do not suggest or refer to any stereotypes of any kind.

Do not appear judgmental toward the accuser, accused, or interviewee.

Indicate your understanding by reflecting and asking follow-up questions, but be sure that you are not giving the impression that you agree with or are taking sides with the witness.

Be sure that you understand the meaning of the descriptive words used by the witness. For example, if a witness asserts he was sent a "disgusting" e-mail—ask him to describe it in detail, and ask him what he means by that descriptive word.

Avoid favoritism.

Explore the potential psychological, emotional, physical, and financial impact of the alleged conduct on each witness.

Gather facts, differentiating between hearsay and opinion.

Elicit possible motives.

Collect names of other possible witnesses.

Leave an opening for later discussion in the event that something is forgotten or a situation develops.

If you can do so without putting words in the witnesses' mouths, restate some of the witnesses' statements in order to determine if your understanding is consistent with the witnesses'.

While avoiding any preconceived notions about the parties involved, you should take precautions to confirm the credibility of every interviewee. Here are some questions to ask yourself as you conduct your interviews:

Is there consistency between the claimant's and accused's stories?

Is there consistency regarding the description of unrelated facts?

Does the interviewee have the ability to corroborate the story or explanation with other witnesses or evidence?

Does the interviewee have the ability to corroborate unrelated facts?

Do several witnesses share a consistent testimony?

Is the interviewee believable? Is the testimony logical?

Is the timing of the complaint intentional? Is the
accuser responding to a recent or planned negative
performance warning?

Is the interviewee sending consistent verbal
and behavioral signals? Evaluate demeanor,
distributing importance as follows: words (10%),
voice tone (40%), and body language (50%).

During the interview, don't be afraid to pause and look
back through your notes. Take your time. Silence need not
be awkward, and the interviewee will realize that you are
trying to be as thorough as possible. After *each* interview
you must take the time to review and clarify your notes,
update the timeline and your evidence list, and determine
how this new information fits into the general context of the
investigation. Moreover, you will need to understand how
information obtained in the interview you just completed
may be relevant to your next and later interviews. After each
interview you will likely have pages and pages of notes—you
will want to make sure that your notes are clear, orderly, and
are a complete summary of what occurred in the interview.
Therefore, when you schedule your interviews, leave yourself
a little time between each in the event that you run over and
to conduct this post-interview recap.

Do any new questions arise from this interview? Do
you have enough data and other evidence to move on? If

you determine that someone else can effectively answer your questions, then schedule a time to meet or insert the new information into your interview outline for that individual.

5. Documentary and Other Evidence

Make sure you always have copies of relevant organization policies readily available for quick reference, and be sure you have reviewed them prior to your meetings with witnesses. Plan and execute a comprehensive search of the computers, lockers, and files of employees (if necessary). Forms of evidence you may gather include

employee files and evaluations,

incident reports,

memos,

procedure manuals, flow charts, etc.,

correspondence,

e-mail or any other computer files,

managers' files,

notes of any kind,

police reports,

pictures, charts, data, and statistics,

project files, and

performance ratings and criteria.

When gathering such evidence, you may find much of it difficult to retrieve. The organization may be working with forensic experts to retrieve digital files. When requesting evidence, be prepared to explain what you hope the information will provide. What kind of light will the evidence shine on the questions in front of you?

When you have the documentary evidence, be sure to confirm its authenticity with the witnesses where relevant. For example, if an employee is accused of sending out e-mails in violation of company policy, you must present the e-mail to the employee and ask him or her if she recognizes it and, in fact, sent it. It may be possible that someone else gained access to the accused's e-mail account and sent out the e-mails. As you can see, it's not as simple as asking if the accused sent out an e-mail. Did she write it? Did someone else have access to her account? If so, did she ever report this? When was the last time she changed her password? Did she receive similar e-mails from others? By clearly delving into the facts, a seemingly simple investigation can yield a variety of complex issues.

6. Timeline of Events

As you conduct the investigation, you are maintaining a detailed timeline that you created in the beginning. Begin with the initial complaint and reconfirm with other witnesses the timeframes presented by the accused. It is not uncommon for a complainant to assert that inappropriate behavior took place over a long period of time. You will want to confirm this information, and the timeline will provide reference points in your investigation, often revealing a level of clarity that will help you sort through the volume of materials and facts you collect. This will prove to be an excellent self-evaluation tool and comprehensive review of the investigation.

7. Preserve Evidence

Safeguard all evidence. Make copies of paper documents, and print hard copies of all electronic data from computers, PDAs, etc. Make recordings of relevant voicemails and other verbal communication, and create transcripts where possible. Explore with witnesses what may be stored off-site, electronically or otherwise—in a shoebox at an employee's home or in his personal home computer.

Yes, erased data can be restored, but often times recovering encrypted or hidden files is time-consuming, complex, and can be very costly. There are no guarantees, so be prepared for the worst. Back up everything digitally and in hard-copy format.

8. Confirm Evidence

Never take evidence on good faith. Confirm and reconfirm everything that you hear. Always consider the reliability of a source, and be aware of any manipulation, tampering or other motives on the part of witnesses.

9. Reaching a Conclusion

Before making a final decision, review your case thoroughly. Consider the credibility of accused, claimant, and witnesses. Outside of the interview, what are the reputations of these individuals? Are they honest or biased? Did each individual's story corroborate the others? Does the accused have a history of misconduct? How plausible is the scenario?

If you believe the claimant had a legitimate complaint, determine whether or not there was an actual violation of policy. Some behaviors are not explicitly prohibited by company policy.

If remedial action is warranted, follow policy guidelines. The penalty should reflect the level and frequency of the misconduct, the accused's knowledge of rules, precedents, and political and relationship elements.

What if your findings are inconclusive? Consider the amount of data you collected over the span of the investigation. Was there truly enough to draw a conclusion? Can you spot any holes or errors in your process? Also, identify any inconsistencies on your part; did you treat every party the same way? Avoid a half-baked investigation and you will always come to a conclusion about which you can feel confident.

10. Confronting the Accused

If you conclude that the accused did, in fact, violate rules of conduct, then you must confront him or her and discuss your findings. Be explicit about the factors that contributed to your decision. Then, listen. The accuser may have further explanation or allege that you are biased in favor of the complainant. These are serious issues, so be prepared to respond. Your timeline and notes are a great reference for you as you explain all the steps that lead you to your conclusion.

Some organizations mince words when it comes to communication with the accused. For example, some hesitate to specifically detail the complaint. Thus, instead of telling the accused exactly what statement or words he or she is accused of speaking, some seek to brush over the details by telling the accused that he is accused of saying something inappropriate. They do this under the guise of ensuring the confidentiality of the complainant. Unfortunately, however, all the accused knows is that someone alleged he said something "inappropriate"; he doesn't know what it is, nor who accused him, Next the employer typically shoves a policy at the accused, asks him to sign it and says "don't do it again." Obviously, I am not a fan of this approach unless there truly is a valid reason for not detailing the allegations with the accused—such as a potential for violence or retaliation. When the details are not shared with the accused, he or she has no way of understanding how a statement he or she made could have been found to be a violation of policy. Moreover, this approach does not give the accused an opportunity to defend him or herself and to present additional relevant facts. In fact, the accuser may be lying.

If you cannot corroborate the accusations, you must still provide feedback to the accused. Tell him or her that the results were inconclusive. Reaffirm the company's relevant policies (i.e., on discrimination, retaliation and harassment), and be sure he or she understands.

11. Follow Up

Eventually the investigation will end, I promise. But now what do you do? First, go back to the beginning, and look to the purpose of your investigation. Either draft a report summarizing the entire investigation, or provide an oral report. Then, file all of your notes and evidence along with that report. If something should come up later, or if another complaint is filed that involves the same parties, your files will be valuable.

Ensure that an appropriate penalty is in place if there has been misconduct, and document any remedial action. Review the policies and procedures, and revise them if necessary. Implement any changes right away. Make sure all employees are aware of changes and that the new procedures are adequate.

Second, evaluate the investigation; double-check for errors and skipped steps. Then, assess yourself on every aspect of the investigation. Was your strategy methodical, and did you execute the plan well? Can you explain your actions—why you did what you did, when you did it? Make note of the things you should improve. Yes, there will be steps that you can improve upon.

Last, follow up with the complainant at some future point in time to ensure that he or she has not been the victim further misconduct. You will want to document this follow up in the investigation file. For example, if the accusation was that the accused made inappropriate comments and solicitations of the complainant, confirm at some later point in time that these have stopped.

12. Communicating Results and Providing Feedback to the Claimant and the Accused

Confronting the accused has its own set of dilemmas. Approaching someone with a conclusion that he or she has violated policy can be awkward for both parties. Therefore, you should prepare a statement that you will make to the accused that clearly identifies the policy violation and the behavior that was inappropriate. You will further want to reaffirm relevant company policies. You should also prepare a statement that you will make to others on a need-to-know basis; this may include management in the area where the allegation took place.

With regard to the complainant, you will want to advise him or her that the investigation is completed and that there were or were not conclusive findings. You will also want to reaffirm the company's relevant policies (such as harassment, discrimination and retaliation) and invite the accuser to come forward again if anything happens in the future. There is no need for you to communicate the nature and type of adverse action taken against the accused if the allegations are found to be true. Suffice to say that all you need to do is state to the claimant that you have taken the appropriate steps to prevent such conduct in the future.

5

The FACT Act and Its Effect on Workplace Investigations

Much has been written on the effect of the Fair and Accurate Credit Transaction Act (FACT Act). Those involved in investigating employee misconduct had been stymied by the Federal Trade Commission's (FTC) interpretation of the requirements of the Fair Credit Reporting Act (FCRA) since the dreaded "Vail Letter" of 1999. The FCRA recognizes two types of reports. The first, consumer reports, are written or oral communications from a consumer reporting agency that bear upon an individual's character, credit-worthiness, general reputation, personal characteristics or mode of living, and are used as a factor in determining eligibility for employment. The second, investigative consumer reports, are prepared by a consumer reporting agency and include the same information, some of which may be gathered from interviews with friends and associates of the individual. Basically, an investigative consumer report involves personal interviews and a consumer report does not.

Until the Vail Letter, the law applied generally to applicants for employment who were subjected to detailed background investigations. The employer was required to obtain advance consent from the applicant, and certain disclosures were required for documents separate from the application for employment. In the event that an employee was penalized for misconduct, the employer was required, among other things, to provide a detailed copy of the misconduct report to the individual. In addition, the employer was required to wait a period of time before taking the adverse action.

In the Vail Letter, an attorney for the Federal Trade Commission (FTC) interpreted the law to require employers who used third parties to investigate allegations of misconduct to comply with the requirements of the FCRA, deeming them "investigative consumer reports" under the law. This meant that employers were now required to seek *consent* from the accused to conduct an investigation. In addition, employers were required to provide the individual with a *full, detailed report* of the investigation prior to taking adverse action.

The FACT Act amended certain provisions of the FCRA and went into effect on March 31, 2004. Specifically, the law changes those requirements, ensuring that employers can conduct a fair and impartial investigation without compromising confidentiality and the investigatory process.

FACT Act Summary

Under the new law, certain investigations of misconduct and alleged violations of employer-written policies are no longer considered investigative consumer reports. Section 603 of the Fair Credit Reporting Act (15 U.S.C. 1681a) was specifically amended to exclude certain communications ("reports") for employee investigations. A report would not be considered an investigative consumer report subject to disclosure rules if the communication is made in connection with the investigation of the following:

(i) Suspected misconduct relating to employment; or

(ii) Compliance with Federal, State, or local laws and regulations, the rules of a self-regulatory organization, or any pre-existing written policies of the employer.

The following also apply:

(i) The communication must not be made for the purpose of investigating a consumer's creditworthiness, credit standing, or credit capacity; and

(ii) The communication must not be provided to any person except

   a. to the employer or an agent of the employer;

   b. to any federal or state officer, agency, or department, or any officer, agency, or department of a unit of general local government;

    c. to any self-regulatory organization with regulatory authority over the activities of the employer or employee;

    d. as otherwise required by law; or

    e. pursuant to section 608 of the FACT Act.

Regarding subsequent disclosure, the following apply:

(i) After taking any adverse action based in whole or in part on a communication, the employer must disclose to the employee a summary containing the nature and substance of the communication upon which the adverse action is based, except that the sources of information acquired solely for use in preparing what would be, but for subsection (d)(2)(D), an investigative consumer report need not be disclosed.

(ii) The term 'self-regulatory organization' includes any self-regulatory organization (as defined in section 3(a)(26) of the Securities Exchange Act of 1934), any entity established under Title I of the Sarbanes-Oxley Act of 2002, any board of trade designated by the Commodity Futures Trading Commission, and any futures association registered with such Commission.

This means that with the use of outside investigators or attorneys, employers no longer have to obtain consent from the accused employee prior to conducting the investigation. In addition, employers are no longer required to provide a detailed report to the individual containing sensitive employee information and the names of interviewed parties. However, employers are required to provide the accused with a summary of the investigation, but may omit these sensitive details. In addition, the employer no longer has to provide this summary prior to taking adverse action. Thus, if the results of the investigation warrant an employee termination, the employer may take that action and provide the summary report after.

6

The Top Ten Investigation Tips

Workplace Investigations: Tip # 1
Scribes, Note-takers, and Transcripts in an Investigation

When conducting an investigation, investigators often try to capture everything that was said by asking an administrative person to take notes during the interview. Sometimes, the investigator will go so far as to ask the other person to play the part of stenographer and record every single word. While I've previously recommended the virtue of recording and note-taking, there are several issues that must be considered:

1. Be very careful with a note-taker present. The note-taker may misquote something or omit something entirely. If the document that the note-taker prepared is offered as evidence and is incomplete or inaccurate, the investigation can be called into

question. Also, opponents can further challenge the notes by claiming that statements or incidents that do not appear in the document never actually occurred.

2. The second problem with the note-taker is that the interview becomes double-teamed. Having employees open up is difficult enough. With the appearance of two against one, making an interviewee comfortable is even more difficult.

My recommendation: As a matter of standard practice, the interviewer should take his or her own notes. Often, these notes may be bullet points to help the investigator draft the report, and are therefore not a complete "transcript" of the interview. Draft your summary report IMMEDIATELY after the investigation while your memory is still clear. The report should adequately describe what occurred in the interview, taking into account that the notes may be incomplete.

Workplace Investigations: Tip # 2
The Purpose of an Investigation

When internal management learns of alleged employee misconduct, they respond with an internal investigation. However, the process of learning the facts, drawing conclusions, and doling out discipline are really three distinct areas. For example, when someone is accused of discrimination or harassment in the workplace by a fellow employee, the human resource professional or management will usually conduct the investigation, draw conclusions, and handle discipline. As

I've stated earlier, the problem with this approach is that one individual may play the role of fact finder, judge, and jury.

When facing an investigation in your organization, my suggestion is to think of each part separately. If you go into an investigation already thinking about how you're going to discipline the accused if he or she is found guilty of a policy violation, you're headed in the wrong direction. Your job is to gather the facts objectively and as fairly as possible. Someone else should be the judge and the jury. By allowing yourself to play all three roles, you risk losing objectivity.

Workplace Investigations: Tip # 3
Confidentiality

The subject of confidentiality in investigations is worthy of several discussions, as there are a variety of issues. For our purposes, imagine the following scenario: an employee feels he is the victim of discrimination or feels that he is being mistreated in some way in the workplace. He approaches a member of management and says, "Something is bothering me, but I don't want you to tell anyone." The manager has two choices:

1. The first is the *wrong* choice. That would be to tell the employee, "Don't tell me, because if you do, I'll have to report this to Human Resources." Why is this a bad option? Because now the employer is aware of a problem and has chosen to do nothing. During the deposition, plaintiff counsel will ask the manager about his conversation with the employee. The supervisor will be portrayed as disinterested

and self-serving even though he may have only been trying to maintain confidentiality at the request of the employee.

2. The right option is to advise the employee that one of a manager's obligations is to attempt to resolve issues that may arise in the workplace. (After all, aren't managers supposed to help foster a productive environment free of misconduct?) He should encourage the employee to discuss his concerns and remind him that management has a responsibility to look into the matter further and report to Human Resources. He should try to put the employee at ease and work diligently to help to resolve the problem. In the event the employee still does not want to talk, then the supervisor should follow the guidelines established by the company—which are typically to inform Human Resources. A manager who has taken this route has no fear of something coming back to haunt him, because he has taken the necessary steps to help the employee and reached out to Human Resources to ensure that there is follow-up.

Workplace Investigations: Tip # 4
What the EEOC Says About Investigations

Many people wonder where to find the guidance provided by the Equal Employment Opportunity Commission (EEOC) on the subject of workplace investigations. The following is what the EEOC will be looking for when conducting an investigation of a claim:

1. The employer should set up a process for a *"prompt, thorough, and impartial"* investigation.

2. A necessary investigation "should be launched immediately."

3. The employer should be prepared to "undertake intermediate measures before completing the investigation to ensure that further harassment does not occur."

4. The employer should "ensure that the individual who conducts the investigation will objectively gather and consider the relevant facts...and should be well-trained in the skills that are required for interviewing witnesses and evaluating credibility."

Workplace Investigations: Tip # 5
Whether or Not to Launch an Investigation

Based upon Security and Exchange Commission (SEC) and Department of Justice assessments of companies' actions, failing to conduct a necessary investigation can lead to disastrous consequences. When deciding whether or not to initiate an investigation, the credibility of the complaint is crucial. My advice: take every claim very seriously, and dismiss the issue only if further investigation reveals a *significant* lack of credibility on the part of the claimant. If in doubt, go forward with an investigation. Better safe than sorry.

Workplace Investigations: Tip # 6
What to do with the file?

You've interviewed your witnesses, reviewed your evidence, and drafted a memo to the employees in question. You now have a presumably large file including witness statements and various notes and reports. Here is what you should do:

1. Take the notes that are not complete, summarize them, and put them into a logical format. Dispose of the scribble. This presumes that your detailed summary is intended to be a complete overview of the investigation.

2. Make sure you have everything you need in the file to document your actions. Include any information upon which you based your interviews and questions.

3. Put the file in a *separate, locked* cabinet away from the employee file. The next time you have a complaint, the files in this cabinet will be a reference. You will be able to determine quickly if any of the accused employees have a history and will be able to review past investigations for precedents and procedures.

Workplace Investigations: Tip # 7
After you have destroyed your rough-draft notes, how can you prove that the summary report really is a truthful summary of the investigation?

There is a potential for plaintiff's counsel to have a field day with this. The internal human resource person is naturally in a position to be challenged, based upon the premise that he or she is not truly objective. I know one plaintiff's attorney who referred to the internal investigation as one big "whitewash." Opposing counsel may believe and attempt to prove that an investigation conducted by insiders is actually an attempt to cover up as much as possible.

Here is your defense against such an accusation: Those of us who conduct investigations build our reputations on a history of being objective and not being beholden to others. In other words, I don't care what I learn in the investigation, as long as I'm getting the truth. I have no stake in the outcome.

Regarding investigatory notes, I have, unfortunately, seen them do more harm than good. For example, I have seen people take notes for some, but not all, interviewees. I have seen some notes typewritten, some handwritten, some written on hotel napkins, etc. At the end of the day, an inept investigator cannot recall who was interviewed about which subjects, the order of witnesses, or the duration of each interview. Worst of all, he or she cannot explain inconsistencies in the interviews. The result is that the investigation looks shoddy and the investigator comes under suspicion. The only way to avoid being challenged on your report is to be as thorough as possible, 100% of the time. Have a consistent process and procedure that you follow, and be able to explain why you did what you did when you did it.

Workplace Investigations: Tip # 8
The Uncooperative Witness

In the course of your investigations you will undoubtedly run into a witness who does not want to participate. What do you do? First, never prevent the witness from leaving if he or she does not want to participate. Explain the importance of participating and that you are trying to obtain the facts. However, if he or she wants to leave, you must oblige. Second, be sure to remind the witness about the nonretaliation provisions of your policy (resistance is sometimes based upon fear of retaliation from others for participating in the investigation). If the resistance is because the witness does not want to "rat" on a friend, inform the witness that as the gatherer of facts, you need to obtain as much information as you can.

You should also be sure that your policies require employees to participate in investigations. If the employee continues to refuse, you can explain that refusal is a violation of the policy and that the employee can and will be subject to discipline.

Workplace Investigations: Tip # 9
When to look at an employee file

Looking at a file too early in the investigation may sway the investigator's perception of the facts. By reviewing a file too late, the investigation may be hampered by the delay in receiving relevant information. Listen carefully to the claim and decide if employee history is relevant to your next step. Often, you will find that you have no choice but to review the employee's file.

Whatever your decision, be sure you can explain why you chose a particular time to check the file. All too often, when the investigation is challenged, the investigator cannot explain why he or she made certain decisions. This damages the credibility of the investigation and the investigator. Consistency and careful decision-making along the way will make all the difference.

Workplace Investigations: Tip #10
Avoiding Defamation Claims

I often hear of human resource professionals or other managers being dragged into litigation. Sometimes a human resource representative is being sued personally; sometimes he or she is abandoned by an employer who, during the heat of litigation, states that the human resource professional's actions were contrary to policy or inappropriate.

To protect yourself against defamation,

document everything;

carefully consider every step of your strategy to make sure you are acting in accordance with policy;

review your responsibilities with management;

hold termination and disciplinary meetings in a private location;

have a witness present for sensitive conversations; and

and once again, **document everything**.

Conclusion

I used to believe that conducting the investigations for my company was totally my responsibility as a human resource professional. Believing I was competent and could be neutral, I had always been taught that being the investigator was an appropriate role for the internal human resource professional.

All legal reasons aside, I began to reconsider that belief when I was involved in a highly politically charged investigation at one of my companies. I found that, upon learning of the allegation, major sectors of the organization took competing sides. The very fact that an investigation had to take place resulted in incredible opposition by some powerful players in the organization. Who was stuck in the middle? Me.

That incident became a turning point for me, and I began to question the traditional approach to investigations. I now believe that the human resource professional within a company is not necessarily solely responsible for all workplace investigations. In many situations, outside investigators and supervising counsel are necessary. The human resource staff, does, however, have an obligation to determine the extent of their role in an investigation, as well as develop a comprehensive plan for workplace investigations.

That being said, conducting a workplace investigation is a significant undertaking. The key to your success as an investigator lies in your willingness to do some really hard work up front. A solid investigation is dependent on the investigator's preparation for every possible scenario. If you make an effort to lay sufficient groundwork, your investigation will flow smoothly.

The bottom line is this: Focus on the plan. Do not concern yourself with the various possible outcomes of the investigation. Your strategy should function as a formula for the investigation to follow. Your role, whether you are the chief investigator or not, is to ensure that your company provides a thorough, fair, and efficient investigation.

Appendix

Equal Employment Opportunity Commission's Enforcement Guidance on Vicarious Employer Liability for Unlawful Harassment by Supervisors

Enforcement Guidance on Vicarious Employer Liability for Unlawful Harassment by Supervisors

I. Introduction

In *Burlington Industries, Inc. v. Ellerth,* 118 S. Ct. 2257 (1998), and *Faragher v. City of Boca Raton,* 118 S. Ct. 2275 (1998), the Supreme Court made clear that employers are subject to vicarious liability for unlawful harassment by supervisors. The standard of liability set forth in these decisions is premised on two principles: 1) an employer is responsible for the acts of its supervisors, and 2) employers should be encouraged to prevent harassment and employees should be encouraged to avoid or limit the harm from harassment. In order to accommodate these principles, the Court held that an employer is always liable for a supervisor's harassment if it culminates in a tangible employment action. However, if it does not, the employer may be able to avoid liability or limit damages by establishing an affirmative defense that includes two necessary elements:

(a) the employer exercised reasonable care to prevent
and correct promptly any harassing behavior, and

(b) the employee unreasonably failed to take advantage
of any preventive or corrective opportunities
provided by the employer or to avoid harm
otherwise.

While the *Faragher* and *Ellerth* decisions addressed sexual harassment, the Court's analysis drew upon standards set forth in cases involving harassment on other protected bases. Moreover, the Commission has always taken the position that the same basic standards apply to all types of prohibited harassment.[1] Thus, the standard of liability set forth in the decisions applies to all forms of unlawful harassment. (See Section II, below.)

Harassment remains a pervasive problem in American workplaces. The number of harassment charges filed with the EEOC and state fair employment practices agencies has risen significantly in recent years. For example, the number of sexual harassment charges has increased from 6,883 in fiscal year 1991 to 15,618 in fiscal year 1998. The number of racial harassment charges rose from 4,910 to 9,908 charges in the same time period.

While the anti-discrimination statutes seek to remedy discrimination, their primary purpose is to prevent violations. The

---

[1] *See, e.g.,* 29 C.F.R. § 1604.11 n.1 ("The principles involved here continue to apply to race, color, religion, or national origin."); EEOC Compliance Manual Section 615.11(a) (BNA) 615:0025 ("Title VII law and agency principles will guide the determination of whether an employer is liable for age harassment by its supervisors, employees, or non-employees").

Supreme Court, in *Faragher* and *Ellerth*, relied on Commission guidance which has long advised employers to take all necessary steps to prevent harassment.[2] The new affirmative defense gives credit for such preventive efforts by an employer, thereby "implement[ing] clear statutory policy and complement[ing] the Government's Title VII enforcement efforts."[3]

The question of liability arises only after there is a determination that unlawful harassment occurred. Harassment does not violate federal law unless it involves discriminatory treatment on the basis of race, color, sex, religion, national origin, age of forty or older, disability, or protected activity under the anti-discrimination statutes. Furthermore, the anti-discrimination statutes are not a "general civility code."[4] Thus, federal law does not prohibit simple teasing, offhand comments, or isolated incidents that are not "extremely serious."[5] Rather, the conduct must be "so objectively offensive as to alter the 'conditions' of the victim's employment."[6] The conditions of employment are altered only if the harassment culminated in a tangible employment action or was sufficiently severe or pervasive to create

---

[2] *See* 1908 Guidelines at 29 C.F.R. § 1604.11(f) and Policy Guidance on Current Issues of Sexual Harassment, Section E, 8 FEP Manual 405:6699 (Mar. 19, 1990), *quoted in Faragher*, 118 S. Ct. at 2292.

[3] *Faragher*, 118 S. Ct. at 2292.

[4] *Oncale v. Sundowner Offshore Services, Inc.*, 118 S. Ct. 998, 1002 (1998).

[5] *Faragher*, 118 S. Ct. at 2283. However, when isolated incidents that are not "extremely serious" come to the attention of management, appropriate corrective action should still be taken so that they do not escalate. *See* Section V(C)(1)(a), below.

[6] *Oncale*, 118 S. Ct. at 1003.

a hostile work environment.[7] Existing Commission guidance on the standards for determining whether challenged conduct rises to the level of unlawful harassment remains in effect.

This document supersedes previous Commission guidance on the issue of vicarious liability for harassment by supervisors.[8] The Commission's long-standing guidance on employer liability for harassment by coworkers remains in effect—an employer is liable if it knew or should have known of the misconduct, unless it can show that it took immediate and appropriate corrective action.[9] The standard is the same in the case of non-employees, but the employer's control over such individuals' misconduct is considered.[10]

---

[7] Some previous Commission documents classified harassment as either "quid pro quo" or hostile environment. However, it is now more useful to distinguish between harassment that results in a tangible employment action and harassment that creates a hostile work environment, since that dichotomy determines whether the employer can raise the affirmative defense to vicarious liability. Guidance on the definition of "tangible employment action" appears in Section IV(B), below.

[8] The guidance in this document applies to federal sector employers, as well as all other employers covered by the statutes enforced by the Commission.

[9] 29 C.F.R. § 1604.11(d).

[10] The Commission will rescind Subsection 1604.11(c) of the 1980 Guidelines on Sexual Harassment, 29 C.F.R. § 1604.11(c). In addition, the following Commission guidance is no longer in effect: Subsection D of the 1990 Policy Statement on Current Issues in Sexual Harassment ("Employer Liability for Harassment by Supervisors"), EEOC Compliance Manual (BNA) N:4050–58 (3/19/90); and EEOC Compliance Manual Section 615.3(c) (BNA) 6:15-0007-0008.
The remaining portions of the 1980 Guidelines, the 1990 Policy Statement, and Section 615 of the Compliance Manual remain in effect. Other Commission guidance on harassment also remains in effect, including the Enforcement Guidance on *Harris v. Forklift Sys., Inc.*, EEOC Compliance Manual (BNA) N:4071 (3/8/94) and the Policy Guidance on Employer Liability for Sexual Favoritism, EEOC Compliance Manual (BNA) N:5051 (3/19/90).

II. The Vicarious Liability Rule Applies to Unlawful Harassment on All Covered Bases

The rule in *Ellerth* and *Faragher* regarding vicarious liability applies to harassment by supervisors based on race, color, sex (whether or not of a sexual nature[11]), religion, national origin, protected activity,[12] age, or disability.[13] Thus, employers should establish anti-harassment policies

---

[11] Harassment that is targeted at an individual because of his or her sex violates Title VII even if it does not involve sexual comments or conduct. Thus, for example, frequent, derogatory remarks about women could constitute unlawful harassment even if the remarks are not sexual in nature. *See* 1990 Policy Guidance on Current Issues of Sexual Harassment, Subsection C(4) ("sex-based harassment—that is, harassment not involving sexual activity or language—may also give rise to Title VII liability...if it is 'sufficiently patterned or pervasive' and directed at employees because of their sex").

[12] "Protected activity" means opposition to discrimination or participation in proceedings covered by the anti-discrimination statutes. Harassment based on protected activity can constitute unlawful retaliation. *See* EEOC Compliance Manual Section 8 ("Retaliation") (BNA) 614:001 (May 20, 1998).

[13] For cases applying *Ellerth* and *Faragher* to harassment on different bases, *see Hafford v. Seidner*, 167 F.3d 1074, 1080 (6th Cir. 1999) (religion and race); *Breeding v. Arthur J. Gallagher and Co.*, 164 F.3d 1151, 1158 (8th Cir. 1999) (age); *Allen v. Michigan Department of Corrections*, 165 F.3d 405, 411 (6th Cir.1999) (race); *Richmond-Hopes v. City of Cleveland*, No. 97-3595, 1998 WL 808222 at *9 (6th Cir. Nov. 16, 1998) (unpublished) (retaliation); *Wright-Simmons v. City of Oklahoma City*, 155 F.3d 1264, 1270 (10th Cir. 1998) (race); *Gotfryd v. Book Covers, Inc.*, No. 97 C 7696, 1999 WL 20925 at *5 (N.D. Ill. Jan 7, 1999) (national origin). *See also Wallin v. Minnesota Department of Corrections*, 153 F.3d 681, 687 (8th Cir. 1998) (assuming without deciding that ADA hostile environment claims are modeled after Title VII claims) *cert. denied*, 119 S. Ct. 1141 (1999).

and complaint procedures covering all forms of unlawful harassment.[14]

III. Who Qualifies as a Supervisor?

A. Harasser in Supervisory Chain of Command

An employer is subject to vicarious liability for unlawful harassment if the harassment was committed by "a supervisor with immediate (or successively higher) authority over the employee."[15] Thus, it is critical to determine whether the person who engaged in unlawful harassment had supervisory authority over the complainant.

The federal employment discrimination statutes do not contain or define the term "supervisor."[116] The statutes make employers liable for the discriminatory acts of their

---

[14] The majority's analysis in both *Faragher* and *Ellerth* drew upon the liability standards for harassment on other protected bases. It is, therefore, clear that the same standards apply. *See Faragher,* 118 S. Ct. at 2283 (in determining appropriate standard of liability for sexual harassment by supervisors, Court "drew upon cases recognizing liability for discriminatory harassment based on race and national origin"); *Ellerth,* 118 S. Ct. at 2268 (Court imported concept of "tangible employment action" in race, age and national origin discrimination cases for resolution of vicarious liability in sexual harassment cases). *See also* cases cited in n.13, above.

[15] *Ellerth,* 118 S. Ct. at 2270; *Faragher,* 118 S. Ct. at 2293.

[16] Numerous statutes contain the word "supervisor," and some contain definitions of the term. *See, e.g.,* 12 U.S.C. § 1813(r) (definition of "State bank supervisor" in legislation regarding Federal Deposit Insurance Corporation); 29 U.S.C. § 152(11) (definition of "supervisor" in National Labor Relations Act); 42 U.S.C. § 8262(2) (definition of "facility energy supervisor" in Federal Energy Initiative legislation). The definitions vary depending on the purpose and structure of each statute. The definition of the word "supervisor" under other statutes does not control, and is not affected by, the meaning of that term under the employment discrimination statutes.

"agents,"[17] and supervisors are agents of their employers. However, agency principles "may not be transferable in all their particulars" to the federal employment discrimination statutes.[18] The determination of whether an individual has sufficient authority to qualify as a "supervisor" for purposes of vicarious liability cannot be resolved by a purely mechanical application of agency law.[19] Rather, the purposes of the anti-discrimination statutes and the reasoning of the Supreme Court decisions on harassment must be considered.

The Supreme Court, in *Faragher* and *Ellerth*, reasoned that vicarious liability for supervisor harassment is appropriate because supervisors are aided in such misconduct by the authority that the employers delegated to them.[20] Therefore, that authority must be of a sufficient magnitude so as to assist the harasser explicitly or implicitly in carrying out the harassment. The determination as to whether a harasser had such authority is based on his or her job function rather than job title (e.g., "team leader") and must be based on the specific facts.

---

[17] *See* 42 U.S.C. 2220e(a) (Title VII); 29 U.S.C. 630(b) (ADEA); and 42 U.S.C. § 12111(5)(A) (ADA) (all defining "employer" as including any agent of the employer).

[18] *Meritor Savings Bank, FSB v. Vinson*, 477 U.S. 57, 72 (1986); *Faragher*, 118 S. Ct. at 2290 n.3; *Ellerth*, 118 S. Ct. at 2266.

[19] *See Faragher*, 118. S. Ct. at 2288 (analysis of vicarious liability "calls not for a mechanical application of indefinite and malleable factors set forth in the Restatement...but rather an inquiry into the reasons that would support a conclusion that harassing behavior ought to be held within the scope of a supervisor's employment...") and at 2290 n.3 (agency concepts must be adapted to the practical objectives of the anti-discrimination statutes).

[20] *Faragher*, 118 S. Ct. at 2290; *Ellerth*, 118 S. Ct. at 2269.

An individual qualifies as an employee's "supervisor" if: the individual has authority to undertake or recommend tangible employment decisions affecting the employee; or the individual has authority to direct the employee's daily work activities.

1. Authority to Undertake or Recommend Tangible Employment Actions

An individual qualifies as an employee's "supervisor" if he or she is authorized to undertake tangible employment decisions affecting the employee. "Tangible employment decisions" are decisions that significantly change another employee's employment status. (For a detailed explanation of what constitutes a tangible employment action, see Subsection IV(B), below.) Such actions include, but are not limited to, hiring, firing, promoting, demoting, and reassigning the employee. As the Supreme Court stated, "[t]angible employment actions fall within the special province of the supervisor."[21]

An individual whose job responsibilities include the authority to recommend tangible job decisions affecting an employee qualifies as his or her supervisor even if the individual does not have the final say. As the Supreme Court recognized in *Ellerth*, a tangible employment decision "may be subject to review by higher level supervisors."[22] As long as the individual's recommendation is given substantial weight by the final decisionmaker(s), that individual meets the definition of supervisor.

---

[21] *Ellerth*, 118 S. Ct. at 2269.
[22] *Ellerth*, 118 S. Ct. at 2269.

2. Authority to Direct Employee's Daily Work Activities

An individual who is authorized to direct another employee's day-to-day work activities qualifies as his or her supervisor even if that individual does not have the authority to undertake or recommend tangible job decisions. Such an individual's ability to commit harassment is enhanced by his or her authority to increase the employee's workload or assign undesirable tasks and, hence, it is appropriate to consider such a person a "supervisor" when determining whether the employer is vicariously liable.

In *Faragher*, one of the harassers was authorized to hire, supervise, counsel, and discipline lifeguards, while the other harasser was responsible for making the lifeguards' daily work assignments and supervising their work and fitness training.[23] There was no question that the Court viewed them *both* as "supervisors," even though one of them apparently lacked authority regarding tangible job decisions.[24]

---

[23] *Faragher*, 118 S. Ct. at 2280. For a more detailed discussion of the harassers' job responsibilities, *see Faragher*, 864 F. Supp. 1552, 1563 (S.D. Fla. 1994).

[24] *See Grozdanich v. Leisure Hills Health Center*, 25 F. Supp. 2d 953, 973 (D. Minn. 1998) ("it is evident that the Supreme Court views the term 'supervisor' as more expansive than as merely including those employees whose opinions are dispositive on hiring, firing, and promotion"; thus, "charge nurse" who had authority to control plaintiff's daily activities and recommend discipline qualified as "supervisor" and, therefore, rendered employer vicariously liable under Title VII for his harassment of plaintiff, subject to affirmative defense).

An individual who is temporarily authorized to direct another employee's daily work activities qualifies as his or her "supervisor" during that time period. Accordingly, the employer would be subject to vicarious liability if that individual commits unlawful harassment of a subordinate while serving as his or her supervisor.

On the other hand, someone who merely relays other officials' instructions regarding work assignments and reports back to those officials does not have true supervisory authority. Furthermore, someone who directs only a limited number of tasks or assignments would not qualify as a "supervisor." For example, an individual whose delegated authority is confined to coordinating a work project of limited scope is not a "supervisor."

B. Harasser Outside Supervisory Chain of Command

In some circumstances, an employer may be subject to vicarious liability for harassment by a supervisor who does not have actual authority over the employee. Such a result is appropriate if the employee reasonably believed that the harasser had such power.[25] The employee might have such

---

[25] *See Ellerth*, 118 S. Ct. at 2268 ("If, in the unusual case, it is alleged there is a false impression that the actor was a supervisor, when he in fact was not, the victim's mistaken conclusion must be a reasonable one."); *Llampallas v. Mini-Circuit Lab, Inc.*, 163 F.3d 1236, 1247 (11th Cir. 1998) ("Although the employer may argue that the employee had no actual authority to take the employment action against the plaintiff, apparent authority serves just as well to impute liability to the employer for the employee's action.").

a belief because, for example, the chains of command are unclear. Alternatively, the employee might reasonably believe that a harasser with broad delegated powers has the ability to significantly influence employment decisions affecting him or her even if the harasser is outside the employee's chain of command.

If the harasser had no actual supervisory power over the employee, and the employee did not reasonably believe that the harasser had such authority, then the standard of liability for coworker harassment applies.

IV. Harassment by Supervisor That Results in a Tangible Employment Action
A. Standard of Liability

An employer is always liable for harassment by a supervisor on a prohibited basis that culminates in a tangible employment action. No affirmative defense is available in such cases.[26] The Supreme Court recognized that this result is appropriate because an employer acts through its supervisors, and a supervisor's undertaking of a tangible employment action constitutes an act of the employer.[27]

---

[26] Of course, traditional principles of mitigation of damages apply in these cases, as well as all other employment discrimination cases. *See generally Ford Motor Co. v. EEOC,* 458 U.S. 219 (1982).

[27] *Ellerth,* 118 S. Ct. at 2269; *Faragher,* 118 S. Ct. 2284–85. *See also Durham Life Insurance Co. v. Evans,* 166 F.3d 139, 152 (3rd Cir. 1999) ("A supervisor can only take a tangible adverse employment action because of the authority delegated by the employer…and thus the employer is properly charged with the consequences of that delegation.").

B. Definition of "Tangible Employment Action"

A tangible employment action is "a significant change in employment status."[28] Unfulfilled threats are insufficient. Characteristics of a tangible employment action are:[29]

1. A tangible employment action is the means by which the supervisor brings the official power of the enterprise to bear on subordinates, as demonstrated by the following:

    *   it requires an official act of the enterprise;
    *   it usually is documented in official company records;
    *   it may be subject to review by higher level supervisors; and
    *   it often requires the formal approval of the enterprise and use of its internal processes.

2. A tangible employment action usually inflicts direct economic harm.

3. A tangible employment action, in most instances, can only be caused by a supervisor or other person acting with the authority of the company.

---

[28] *Ellerth,* 118. S. Ct. at 2268.
[29] All listed criteria are set forth in *Ellerth,* 118 S. Ct. at 2269.

Examples of tangible employment actions include:[30]
hiring and firing;

- promotion and failure to promote;
- demotion;[31]
- undesirable reassignment;
- a decision causing a significant change in benefits;
- compensation decisions; and
- work assignment.

Any employment action qualifies as "tangible" if it results in a significant change in employment status. For example, significantly changing an individual's duties in his or her existing job constitutes a tangible employment action regardless of whether the individual retains the same salary and

---

[30] All listed examples are set forth in *Ellerth* and/or *Faragher*. *See Ellerth*, 118 S. Ct. at 2268 and 2270; *Faragher*, 118 S. Ct. at 2284, 2291, and 2293.

[31] Other forms of formal discipline would qualify as well, such as suspension. Any disciplinary action undertaken as part of a program of progressive discipline is "tangible" because it brings the employee one step closer to discharge.

benefits.[32] Similarly, altering an individual's duties in a way that blocks his or her opportunity for promotion or salary increases also constitutes a tangible employment action.[33]

On the other hand, an employment action does not reach the threshold of "tangible" if it results in only an insignificant change in the complainant's employment status. For example, altering an individual's job title does not qualify as a tangible employment action if there is no change in salary, benefits, duties, or prestige, and the only effect is a bruised ego.[34] However, if there is a significant change in the status

---

[32] The Commission disagrees with the Fourth Circuit's conclusion in *Reinhold v. Commonwealth of Virginia,* 151 F.3d 172 (4th Cir. 1998), that the plaintiff was not subjected to a tangible employment action where the harassing supervisor "dramatically increased her workload," *Reinhold,* 947 F. Supp. 919, 923 (E.D. Va. 1996), denied her the opportunity to attend a professional conference, required her to monitor and discipline a coworker, and generally gave her undesirable assignments. The Fourth Circuit ruled that the plaintiff had no been subjected to a tangible employment action because she had not "experienced a change in her employment status akin to a demotion or a reassignment entailing significantly different job responsibilities." 151 F.3d at 175. It is the Commission's view that the Fourth Circuit misconstrued *Faragher* and *Ellerth.* While minor changes in work assignments would not rise to the level of tangible job harm, the actions of the supervisor in *Reinhold* were substantial enough to significantly alter the plaintiff's employment status.

[33] *See Durham,* 166 F.3d at 152–53 (assigning insurance salesperson heavy load of inactive policies, which had a severe negative impact on her earnings, and depriving her or her private office and secretary, were tangible employment actions); *Bryson v. Chicago State University,* 96 F.3d 912, 917 (7th Cir. 1996) ("Depriving someone of the building blocks for...a promotion...is just as serious as depriving her of the job itself.").

[34] *See Flaherty v. Gas Research Institute,* 31 F.3d 451, 457 (7th Cir. 1994) (change in reporting relationship requiring plaintiff to report to former subordinate, while maybe bruising plaintiff's ego, did not affect his salary, benefits, and level of responsibility and, therefore, could not be challenged in ADEA claim), *cited in Ellerth,* 118 S. Ct. at 2269.

of the position because the new title is less prestigious and thereby effectively constitutes a demotion, a tangible employment action would be found.[35]

If a supervisor undertakes or recommends a tangible job action based on a subordinate's response to unwelcome sexual demands, the employer is liable and cannot raise the affirmative defense. The result is the same whether the employee rejects the demands and is subjected to an adverse tangible employment action or submits to the demands and consequently obtains a tangible job benefit.[36] Such harassment previously would have been characterized as "quid pro quo." It would be a perverse result if the employer is foreclosed from raising the affirmative defense if its supervisor denies a tangible job benefit based on an employee's rejection of unwelcome sexual demands, but can raise the defense if its supervisor grants a tangible job benefit based on submission to such demands. The Commission rejects such an analysis. In both those situations the supervisor undertakes a tangible employment action on a discriminatory basis. The Supreme Court stated that there must be a significant *change*

---

[35] *See Crady v. Liberty Nat. Bank & Trust Co., of Ind.,* 993 F.2d 132, 136 (7th Cir. 1993) ("A materially adverse change might be indicated by a termination of employment, a demotion evidenced by a decrease in wage or salary, a less distinguished title, a material loss of benefits, significantly diminished material responsibilities, or other indices that might be unique to the particular situation."), *quoted in Ellerth,* 118 S. Ct. at 2268–69.

[36] *See Nichols v. Frank,* 42 F.3d 503, 512–13 (9th Cir. 1994) (employer vicariously liable where its supervisor granted plaintiff's leave requested based on her submission to sexual conduct), *cited in Faragher,* 118 S. Ct. at 2285.

in employment status; it did not require that the change be adverse in order to qualify as tangible.[37]

If a challenged employment action is not "tangible," it may still be considered, along with other evidence, as part of a hostile environment claim that is subject to the affirmative defense. In *Ellerth*, the Court concluded that there was no tangible employment action because the supervisor never carried out his threats of job harm. Ellerth could still proceed with her claim of harassment, but the claim was properly "categorized as a hostile work environment claim which requires a showing of severe or pervasive conduct." 118 S. Ct. at 2265.

C. Link Between Harassment and Tangible Employment Action

When harassment culminates in a tangible employment action, the employer cannot raise the affirmative defense. This sort of claim is analyzed like any other case in which a challenged employment action is alleged to be discriminatory. If the employer produces evidence of a non-discriminatory explanation for the tangible employment action, a determination must be made whether that explanation is a pretext designed to hide a discriminatory motive.

For example, if an employee alleged that she was demoted because she refused her supervisor's sexual advances, a

---

[37] *See Ellerth,* 118 S. Ct. at 2268 and *Faragher,* 118 S. Ct. at 2284 (listed examples of tangible employment actions that included both positive and negative job decisions: hiring *and* firing; promotion *and* failure to promote).

determination would have to be made whether the demotion was because of her response to the advances and, hence, because of her sex. Similarly, if an employee alleges that he was discharged after being subjected to severe or pervasive harassment by his supervisor based on his national origin, a determination would have to be made whether the discharge was because of the employee's national origin.

A strong inference of discrimination will arise whenever a harassing supervisor undertakes or has significant input into a tangible employment action affecting the victim,[38] because it can be "assume[d] that the harasser... could not act as an objective, non-discriminatory decision maker with respect to the plaintiff."[39] However, if the employer produces evidence of a non-discriminatory reason for the action, the employee will have to prove that the asserted reason was a pretext designed to hide the true discriminatory motive.

If it is determined that the tangible action was based on a discriminatory reason linked to the preceding harassment, relief could be sought for the entire pattern of misconduct culminating in the tangible employment action, and

---

[38] The link could be established even if the harasser was not the ultimate decision maker. *See, e.g., Shager v. Upjohn Co.,* 913 F.2d 398, 405 (7th Cir. 1990) (noting that committee rather than the supervisor fired plaintiff, but employer was still liable because committee functioned as supervisor's "cat's paw"), *cited in Ellerth,* 118 S. Ct. at 2269.

[39] *Llampallas,* 163, F.3d at 1247.

no affirmative defense is available.[40] However, the harassment preceding the tangible employment action must be severe or pervasive in order to be actionable.[41] If the tangible employment action was based on a non-discriminatory motive, then the employer would have an opportunity to raise the affirmative defense to a claim based on the preceding harassment.[42]

---

[40] *Ellerth,* 118 S. Ct. at 2270 ("[n]o affirmative defense is available...when the supervisor's harassment culminates in a tangible employment action..."); *Faragher,* 118 S. Ct. at 2293 (same). *See also Durham,* 166 F.3d at 154 ("When harassment becomes adverse employment action, the employer loses the affirmative defense, even if it might have been available before."); *Lissau v. Southern Food Services, Inc.,* 159 F.3d 177, 184 (4th Cir. 1998) (the affirmative defense "is not available in a hostile work environment case when the supervisor takes a tangible employment action against the employee as part of the harassment") (Michael, J., concurring).

[41] *Ellerth,* 118 S. Ct. at 2265. Even if the preceding acts were not severe or pervasive, they still may be relevant evidence in determining whether the tangible employment action was discriminatory.

[42] *See Lissau v. Southern Food Service, Inc.,* 159 F.3d at 182 (if plaintiff could not prove that her discharge resulted from her refusal to submit to her supervisor's sexual harassment, then the defendant could advance the affirmative defense); *Newton v. Caldwell Laboratories,* 156 F.3d 880, 883 (8th Cir. 1998) (plaintiff failed to prove that her rejection of her supervisor's sexual advances was the reason that her request for a transfer was denied and that she was discharged; her claim was, therefore, categorized as one of hostile environment harassment); *Fierro v. Saks Fifth Avenue,* 13 F. Supp.2d 481, 491 (S.D.N.Y. 1998) (plaintiff claimed that his discharge resulted from national origin harassment but court found that he was discharged because of embezzlement; thus, employer could raise affirmative defense as to the harassment preceding the discharge).

V. Harassment by Supervisor That Does Not Result in a Tangible Employment Action

A. *Standard of Liability*

When harassment by a supervisor creates an unlawful hostile environment but does not result in a tangible employment action, the employer can raise an affirmative defense to liability or damages, which it must prove by a preponderance of the evidence. The defense consists of two necessary elements:

(a) the employer exercised reasonable care to prevent and correct promptly any harassment; and

(b) the employee unreasonably failed to take advantage of any preventive or corrective opportunities provided by the employer or to avoid harm otherwise.

B. *Effect of Standard*

If an employer can prove that it discharged its duty of reasonable care and that the employee could have avoided all of the harm but unreasonably failed to do so, the employer will avoid all liability for unlawful harassment.[43] For example, if an employee was subjected to a pattern of disability-based harassment that created an unlawful hostile environment,

---

[43] *See Faragher,* 118, S. Ct. at 2292 ("If the victim could have avoided harm, no liability should be found against the employer who had taken reasonable care.").

but the employee unreasonably failed to complain to management before she suffered emotional harm and the employer exercised reasonable care to prevent and promptly correct the harassment, then the employer will avoid all liability.

If an employer cannot prove that it discharged its duty of reasonable care *and* that the employee unreasonably failed to avoid the harm, the employer will be liable. For example, if unlawful harassment by a supervisor occurred and the employer failed to exercise reasonable care to prevent it, the employer will be liable even if the employee unreasonably failed to complain to management or even if the employer took prompt and appropriate corrective action when it gained notice.[44]

In most circumstances, if employers and employees discharge their respective duties of reasonable care, unlawful harassment will be prevented and there will be no reason to consider questions of liability. An effective complaint procedure "encourages employees to report harassing conduct before it becomes severe or pervasive,"[45] and if an employee

---

[44] *See, e.g., EEOC v. SBS Transit, Inc.*, No. 97-4164, 1998 WL 903833 at *1 (6th Cir. Dec. 18, 1998) (unpublished) (lower court erred when it reasoned that employer liability for sexual harassment is negated if the employer responds adequately and effectively once it has notice of the supervisor's harassment; that standard conflicts with affirmative defense which requires proof that employer "took reasonable care to *prevent* and correct promptly any sexually harassing behavior and that the plaintiff employee unreasonably failed to take advantage of preventive or corrective opportunities provided by the employer").

[45] *Ellerth*, S. Ct. at 2270.

promptly utilizes that procedure, the employer can usually stop the harassment before actionable harm occurs.[46]

In some circumstances, however, unlawful harassment will occur and harm will result despite the exercise of requisite legal care by the employer and employee. For example, if an employee's supervisor directed frequent, egregious racial epithets at him that caused emotional harm virtually from the outset, and the employee promptly complained, corrective action by the employer could prevent further harm but might not correct the actionable harm that the employee already had

---

[46] *See Indest v. Freeman Decorating, Inc.,* 168 F.3d 795, 803 (5th Cir. 1999) ("when an employer satisfies the first element of the Supreme Court's affirmative defense, it will likely forestall its own vicarious liability for a supervisor's discriminatory conduct by nipping such behavior in the bud") (Wiener, J., concurring in *Indest,* 164 F.3d 258 (5th Cir. 1999)). The Commission agrees with Judge Wiener's concurrence in *Indest* that the court in that case dismissed the plaintiff's claims on an erroneous basis. The plaintiff alleged that her supervisor made five crude sexual comments or gestures to her during a week-long convention. She reported the incidents to appropriate management officials who investigated the matter and meted out appropriate discipline. No further incidents of harassment occurred. The court noted that it was "difficult to conclude" that the conduct to which the plaintiff was briefly subjected created an unlawful hostile environment. Nevertheless, the court went on to consider liability. It stated that *Ellerth* and *Faragher* do not apply where the plaintiff quickly resorted to the employer's grievance procedure and the employer took prompt remedial action. In such a case, according to the court, the employer's quick response exempts it from liability. The Commission agrees with Judge Wiener that *Ellerth* and *Fagaher* do control the analysis in such cases, and that an employee's prompt complaint to management forecloses the employer from proving the affirmative defense. However, as Judge Wiener pointed out, an employer's quick remedial action will often thwart the creation of an unlawful hostile environment, rendering any consideration of employer liability unnecessary.

suffered.[47] Alternatively, if an employee complained about harassment before it became severe or pervasive, remedial measures undertaken by the employer might fail to stop the harassment before it reaches an actionable level, even if those measures are reasonably calculated to halt it. In these circumstances, the employer will be liable because the defense requires proof that it exercised reasonable legal care and that the employee unreasonably failed to avoid the harm. While a notice-based negligence standard would absolve the employer of liability, the standard set forth in *Ellerth* and *Faragher* does not. As the Court explained, vicarious liability sets a "more stringent standard" for the employer than the "minimum standard" of negligence theory.[48]

While this result may seem harsh to a law-abiding employer, it is consistent with liability standards under the anti-discrimination statutes which generally make employers responsible for the discriminatory acts of their supervisors.[49]

---

[47] *See Greene v. Dalton,* 164 F.3d 671, 674 (D.C. Cir. 1999) (in order for defendant to avoid all liability for sexual harassment leading to rape of plaintiff, "it must show not merely that [the plaintiff] inexcusably delayed reporting the alleged rape...but that, as a matter of law, a reasonable person in [her] place would have come forward early enough to prevent [the] harassment from becoming 'severe or pervasive'").

[48] *Ellerth,* 118 S. Ct. at 2267.

[49] Under this same principle, it is the Commission's position that an employer is liable for punitive damages if its supervisor commits unlawful harassment or other discriminatory conduct with malice or with reckless indifference to the employee's federally protected rights. (The Supreme Court will determine the standard for awarding punitive damages in *Kolstad v. American Dental Association,* 119 S. Ct. 401 (1998) (granting certiorari)). The test for imposition of punitive damages is the mental state of the harasser, not of higher-level officials. This approach furthers the remedial and deterrent objectives of the anti-discrimination statutes and is consistent with the vicarious liability standard set for the *Faragher* and *Ellerth.*

If, for example, a supervisor rejects a candidate for promotion because of national origin-based bias, the employer will
be liable regardless of whether the employee complained
to higher management and regardless of whether higher
management had any knowledge about the supervisor's
motivation.[50] Harassment is the only type of discrimination
carried out by a supervisor for which an employer can avoid
liability, and that limitation must be construed narrowly.
The employer will be shielded from liability for harassment
by a supervisor only if it proves that it exercised reasonable
care in preventing and correcting the harassment *and* that
the employee unreasonably failed to avoid all of the harm.
If both parties exercise reasonable care, the defense will fail.

In some cases, an employer will be unable to avoid liability completely, but may be able to establish the affirmative defense as a means to limit damages.[51] The defense
only limits damages where the employee reasonably could
have avoided some but not all of the harm from the harassment. In the example above, in which the supervisor used
frequent, egregious racial epithets, an unreasonable delay
by the employee in complaining could limit damages but
not eliminate liability entirely. This is because a reasonably

---

[50] Even if higher management proves that evidence is discovered after-
the-fact would have justified the supervisor's action, such evidence can
only limit remedies, not eliminate liability. *McKennon v. Nashville Banner
Publishing Co.,* 513 U.S. 352, 360–62 (1995).
[51] *See Faragher,* 118 S. Ct. at 2293, and *Ellerth,* 118 S. Ct. at 2270 (affirmative
defense operates either to eliminate liability or limit damages).

prompt complaint would have reduced, but not eliminated, the actionable harm.[52]

C. *First Prong of Affirmative Defense: Employer's Duty to Exercise Reasonable Care*

The first prong of the affirmative defense requires a showing by the employer that it undertook reasonable care to prevent and promptly correct harassment. Such reasonable care generally requires an employer to establish, disseminate, and enforce an anti-harassment policy and complaint procedure and to take other reasonable steps to prevent and correct harassment. The steps described below are not mandatory requirements—whether or not an employer can prove that it exercised reasonable care depends on the particular factual circumstances and, in some cases, the nature of the employer's workforce. Small employers may be able to effectively prevent and correct harassment through informal means, while larger employers may have to institute more formal mechanisms.[53]

There are no "safe harbors" for employers based on the written content of policies and procedures. Even the best policy and complaint procedure will not alone satisfy the burden of proving reasonable care if, in the particular circumstances of a claim, the employer failed to implement its process

---

[52] *See Faragher,* 118 S. Ct. at 2292 ("if damages could reasonably have been mitigated no award against a liable employer should reward a plaintiff for what her own efforts could have avoided").

[53] See Section V(C)(3) for a discussion of preventive and corrective care by small employers.

effectively.[54] If, for example, the employer has an adequate policy and complaint procedure and properly responded to an employee's complaint of harassment, but management ignored previous complaints by other employees about the same harasser, then the employer has not exercised reasonable care in preventing the harassment.[55] Similarly, if the employer has an adequate policy and complaint procedure but an official failed to carry out his or her responsibility to conduct an effective investigation of a harassment complaint, the employer has not discharged its duty to exercise reasonable care. Alternatively, lack of a formal policy and complaint procedure will not defeat the defense if the employer exercised sufficient care through other means.

1. Policy and Complaint Procedure

It generally is necessary for employers to establish, publicize, and enforce anti-harassment policies and complaint procedures. As the Supreme Court stated,

---

[54] *See Hurley v. Atlantic City Police Dept.*, No. 96-5634, 96-5633, 96-5661, 96-5738, 1999 WL 150301 (3rd Cir. March 18, 1999) (*"Ellerth* and *Faragher* do not, as the defendants seem to assume, focus mechanically on the formal existence of a sexual harassment policy, allowing an absolute defense to a hostile work environment claim whenever the employer can point to an anti-harassment policy of some sort"; defendant failed to prove affirmative defense where it issued written policies without enforcing them, painted over offensive graffiti every few months only to see it go up again in minutes, and failed to investigate sexual harassment as it investigated and punished other forms of misconduct.).

[55] *See Dees v. Johnson Controls World Services, Inc.*, 168 F.3d 417, 422 (11th Cir. 1999) (employer can be held liable despite its immediate and appropriate corrective action in response to harassment complaint if it had knowledge of the harassment prior to the complaint and took no corrective action).

"Title VII is designed to encourage the creation of anti-harassment policies and effective grievance mechanisms." *Ellerth,* 118 S. Ct. at 2270. While the Court noted that this "is not necessary in every instance as a matter of law,"[56] failure to do so will make it difficult for an employer to prove that it exercised reasonable care to prevent and correct harassment.[57] (See Section V(C)(3), below, for discussion of preventive and corrective measures by small businesses.)

An employer should provide every employee with a copy of the policy and complaint procedure, and redistribute it periodically. The policy and complaint procedure should be written in a way that will be understood by all employees in the employer's workforce.

---

[56] *Ellerth,* 118 S. Ct. at 2270.

[57] A union grievance and arbitration system does not fulfill this obligation. Decision making under such a system addresses the collective interests of bargaining unit members, while decision making under an internal harassment complaint process should focus on the individual complainant's rights under the employer's anti-harassment policy.

An arbitration, mediation, or other alternative dispute resolution process also does not fulfill the employer's duty of due care. The employer cannot discharge its responsibility to investigate complaints of harassment and undertake corrective measures by providing employees with a dispute resolution process. For further discussion of the impact of such procedures on the affirmative defense, see Section V(D)(1)(b), below.

Finally, a federal agency's formal, internal EEO complaint process does not, by itself, fulfill its obligation to exercise reasonable care. That process only addresses complaints of violations of the federal EEO laws, while the Court, in *Ellerth,* made clear that an employer should encourage employees "to report harassing conduct before it becomes severe or pervasive," *Ellerth,* 118 S. Ct. at 2270. Furthermore, the EEO process is designed to assess whether the agency is liable for unlawful discrimination and does not necessarily fulfill the agency's obligation to undertake immediate and appropriate corrective action.

Other measures to ensure effective dissemination of the policy and complaint procedure include posting them in central locations and incorporating them into employee handbooks. If feasible, the employer should provide training to all employees to ensure that they understand their rights and responsibilities.

An anti-harassment policy and complaint procedure should contain, at a minimum, the following elements:

- a clear explanation of prohibited conduct;
- assurance that employees who make complaints of harassment or provide information related to such complaints will be protected against retaliation;
- a clearly described complaint process that provides accessible avenues of complaint;
- assurance that the employer will protect the confidentiality of harassment complaints to the extent possible;
- a complaint process that provides a prompt, thorough, and impartial investigation; and
- assurance that the employer will take immediate and appropriate corrective action when it determines that harassment has occurred.

The above elements are explained in the following subsections.

a. Prohibition Against Harassment

An employer's policy should make clear that it will not tolerate harassment based on sex (with or without sexual conduct), race, color, religion, national origin, age, disability, and protected activity (*i.e.*, opposition to prohibited discrimination or participation in the statutory complaint process). This prohibition should cover harassment by *anyone* in the workplace—supervisors, coworkers, or non-employees.[58] Management should convey the seriousness of the prohibition. One way to do that is for the mandate to "come from the top," *i.e.*, from upper management.

The policy should encourage employees to report harassment *before* it becomes severe or pervasive. While isolated incidents of harassment generally do not violate federal law, a pattern of such incidents may be unlawful. Therefore, to discharge its duty

---

[58] Although the affirmative defense does not apply in cases of harassment by coworkers or non-employees, an employer cannot claim lack of knowledge as a defense to such harassment if it did not make clear to employees that they can bring such misconduct to the attention of management and that such complaints will be addressed. *See Perry v. Ethan Allen*, 115 F.3d 143, 149 (2nd Cir. 1997) ("When harassment is perpetrated by the plaintiff's coworkers, an employer will be liable if the plaintiff demonstrates that 'the employer either provided no reasonable avenue for complaint or new of the harassment but did nothing about it'"), *cited in Faragher*, 118 S. Ct. at 2289. Furthermore, an employer is liable for harassment by a coworker or non-employer if management knew or should have known of the misconduct, unless the employer can show that it took immediate and appropriate correction action. 29 C.F.R. § 1604.11(d). Therefore, the employer should have a mechanism for investigating such allegations and undertaking corrective action, where appropriate.

of preventive care, the employer must make clear to employees that it will stop harassment before it rises to the level of a violation of federal law.

b. Protection Against Retaliation

An employer should make clear that it will not tolerate adverse treatment of employees because they report harassment or provide information related to such complaints. An anti-harassment policy and complaint procedure will not be effective without such an assurance.[59]

Management should undertake whatever measures are necessary to ensure that retaliation does not occur. For example, when management investigates a complaint of harassment, the official who interviews the parties and witnesses should remind these individuals about the prohibition against retaliation. Management also should scrutinize employment decisions affecting the complainant and witnesses during and after the investigation to ensure that such decisions are not based on retaliatory motives.

---

[59] Surveys have shown that a common reason for failure to report harassment to management is fear of retaliation. *See, e.g.,* Louise F. Fitzgerald & Suzanne Swan, "Why Didn't She Just Report Him? The Psychological and Legal Implications of Women's Responses to Sexual Harassment" 51 *Journal of Social Issues* 117, 121–122 (1995) (citing studies). Surveys have also shown that a significant proportion of harassment victims are worse off after complaining. *Id.* at 123–24; *see also* Patricia A. Frazier, "Overview of Sexual Harassment From the Behavioral Science Perspective," paper presented at the American Bar Association National Institute on Sexual Harassment at B-17 (1998) (reviewing studies that show frequency of retaliation after victims confront their harasser or filed formal complaints).

c. *Effective Complaint Process*

An employer's harassment complaint procedure should be designed to encourage victims to come forward. To that end, it should clearly explain the process and ensure that there are no unreasonable obstacles to complaints. A complaint procedure should not be rigid, since that could defeat the goal of preventing and correcting harassment. When an employee complains to management about alleged harassment, the employer is obligated to investigate the allegation regardless of whether it conforms to a particular format or is made in writing.

The complaint procedure should provide accessible points of contact for the initial complaint.[60] A complaint process is not effective if employees are always required to complain first to their supervisors about alleged harassment, since the supervisor may be a harasser.[61] Moreover, reasonable care in preventing and correcting harassment requires an

---

[60] *See Wilson v. Tulsa Junior College*, 164 F.3d 534, 541 (10th Cir. 1998) (complaint process deficient where it permitted employees to bypass the harassing supervisor by complaining to director of personnel services, but the director was inaccessible due to hours of duty and location in separate facility).

[61] *Faragher*, 118 S. Ct. at 2293 (in holding as matter of law that City did not exercise reasonable care to prevent the supervisors' harassment, Court took note of fact that City's policy "did not include any assurance that the harassing supervisors could be bypassed in registering complaints"); *Meritor Savings Bank, FSB v. Vinson*, 471 U.S. 57, 72 (1986).

employer to instruct all supervisors to report complaints of harassment to appropriate officials.[62]

It is advisable for an employer to designate at least one official outside an employee's chain of command to take complaints of harassment. For example, if the employer has an office of human resources, one or more officials in that office could be authorized to take complaints. Allowing an employee to bypass his or her chain of command provides additional assurance that the complaint will be handled in an impartial manner, since an employee who reports harassment by his or her supervisor may feel that officials within the chain of command will more readily believe the supervisor's version of events.

It also is important for an employer's anti-harassment policy and complaint procedure to contain information about the time frames for filing charges of unlawful harassment with the EEOC or state fair employment practice agencies and to explain that the deadline runs from the last date of unlawful harassment, not from the date that the complaint to the

---

[62] *See Wilson,* 164 F.3d at 541 (complaint procedure deficient because it only required supervisors to report "formal" as opposed to "informal" complaints of harassment); *Varner v. National Super Markets Inc.,* 94 F.3d 1209, 1213 (8th Cir. 1996), *cert. denied,* 519 U.S. 1110 (1997) (complaint procedure is not effective if it does not require supervisor with knowledge of harassment to report the information to those in position to take appropriate action).

employer is resolved.[63] While a prompt complaint process should make it feasible for an employee to delay deciding whether to file a charge until the complaint to the employer is resolved, he or she is not required to do so.[64]

d. Confidentiality

An employer should make clear to employees that it will protect the confidentiality of harassment allegations to the extent possible. An employer cannot guarantee complete confidentiality, since it cannot conduct an effective investigation without revealing certain information to the alleged harasser and potential witnesses. However, information about the allegation of harassment should be shared only with those who need to know about it. Records

---

[63] It is particularly important for federal agencies to explain the statute of limitations for filing formal EEO complaints, because the regulatory deadline is only forty-five days and employees may otherwise assume they can wait whatever length of time it takes for management to complete its internal investigation.

[64] If an employer actively misleads an employee into missing the deadline for filing a charge by dragging out its investigation and assuring the employee that the harassment will be rectified, then the employer would be "equitably estopped" from challenging the delay. *See Currier v. Radio Free Europe/Radio Liberty, Inc.*, 159 F.3d 1363, 1368 (D.C. Cir. 1998) ("an employer's affirmatively misleading statements that a grievance will be resolved in the employee's favor can establish an equitable estoppel"); *Miranda v. B & B Cash Grocery Store, Inc.*, 975 F.2d 1518, 1531 (11th Cir. 1992) (tolling is appropriate where plaintiff was led by defendant to believe that the discriminatory treatment would be rectified); *Miller v. Beneficial Management Corp.*, 977 F.2d 834, 845 (3rd Cir. 1992) (equitable tolling applies where employer's own acts or omission has lulled the plaintiff into foregoing prompt attempt to vindicate his rights).

relating to harassment complaints should be kept confidential on the same basis.[65]

A conflict between an employee's desire for confidentiality and the employer's duty to investigate may arise if an employee informs a supervisor about alleged harassment, but asks him or her to keep the matter confidential and take no action. Inaction by the supervisor in such circumstances could lead to employer liability. While it may seem reasonable to let the employee determine whether to pursue a complaint, the employer must discharge its duty to prevent and correct harassment.[66] One mechanism to help avoid such conflicts would be for the employer to set up an informational phone line which employees can use to discuss questions or concerns about harassment on an anonymous basis.[67]

---

[65] The sharing of records about a harassment complaint with prospective employers of the complainant could constitute unlawful retaliation. *See* Compliance Manual Section 8 ("Retaliation"), Subsection IID(2), (BNA) 614:0005 (5/20/98).

[66] One court has suggested that it may be permissible to honor such a request, but that when the harassment is severe, an employer cannot just stand by, even if requested to do so. *Torres v. Pisano,* 116 F.3d 625 (2nd Cir.), *cert. denied,* 118 S. Ct. 563 (1997).

[67] Employers may hesitate to set up such a phone line due to concern that it may create a duty to investigate anonymous complaints, even if based on mere rumor. To avoid any confusion as to whether an anonymous complaint through such a phone line triggers an investigation, the employer should make clear that the person who takes the calls is not a management official and can only answer questions and provide information. An investigation will proceed only if a complaint is made through the internal complaint process or if management otherwise learns about alleged harassment.

e. Effective Investigative Process

An employer should set up a mechanism for a prompt, thorough, and impartial investigation into alleged harassment. As soon as management learns about alleged harassment, it should determine whether a detailed fact-finding investigation is necessary. For example, if the alleged harasser does not deny the accusation, there would be no need to interview witnesses, and the employer could immediately determine appropriate corrective action.

If a fact-finding investigation is necessary, it should be launched immediately. The amount of time that it will take to complete the investigation will depend on the particular circumstances.[68] If, for example, multiple individuals were allegedly harassed, then it will take longer to interview the parties and witnesses.

---

[68] *See, e.g., Van Zant v. KLM Royal Dutch Airlines*, 80 F.3d 708, 715 (2nd Cir. 1996) (employer's response prompt where it began investigation on the day that complaint was made, conducted interviews within two days, and fired the harasser within ten days); *Steiner v. Showboat Operating Co.*, 25 F.3d 1459, 1464 (9th Cir. 1994) (employer's response to complaints inadequate despite eventual discharge of harasser where it did not seriously investigate or strongly reprimand supervisor until after plaintiff filed charge with state FEP agency), *cert. denied*, 513 U.S. 1082 (1995); *Saxton v. AT&T*, 10 F.3d 526, 535 (7th Cir. 1993) (investigation prompt where it was begun one day after complaint and a detailed report was completed two weeks later); *Nash v. Electrospace Systems, Inc.*, 9 F.3d 401, 404 (5th Cir. 1993) (prompt investigation completed within one week); *Juarez v. Ameritech Mobile Communications, Inc.*, 957 F.2d 317, 319 (7th Cir. 1992) (adequate investigation completed within four days).

It may be necessary to undertake intermediate measures before completing the investigation to ensure that further harassment does not occur. Examples of such measures are: making scheduling changes so as to avoid contact between the parties; transferring the alleged harasser; or placing the alleged harasser on non-disciplinary leave with pay pending the conclusion of the investigation. The complainant should not be involuntarily transferred or otherwise burdened, since such measures could constitute unlawful retaliation.

The employer should ensure that the individual who conducts the investigation will objectively gather and consider the relevant facts. The alleged harasser should not have supervisory authority over the individual who conducts the investigation and should not have any direct or indirect control over the investigation. Whoever conducts the investigation should be well trained in the skills that are required for interviewing witnesses and evaluating credibility.

i. Questions to Ask Parties and Witnesses

When detailed fact-finding is necessary, the investigator should interview the complainant, the alleged harasser, and third parties who could reasonably be expected to have relevant information. Information relating to the personal lives of the parties outside the workplace would be relevant only in unusual circumstances. When interviewing the parties and witnesses, the investigator should refrain from offering his or her opinion.

The following are examples of questions that may be appropriate to ask the parties and potential witnesses. Any actual investigation must be tailored to the particular facts.

Questions to Ask the Complainant:

- Who, what, when, where, and how: *Who* committed the alleged harassment? *What* exactly occurred or was said? *When* did it occur and is it still ongoing? *Where* did it occur? *How* often did it occur? *How* did it affect you?
- How did you react? What response did you make when the incident(s) occurred or afterwards?
- How did the harassment affect you? Has your job been affected in any way?
- Are there any persons who have relevant information? Was anyone present when the alleged harassment occurred? Did you tell anyone about it? Did anyone see you immediately after episodes of alleged harassment?
- Did the person who harassed you harass anyone else? Do you know whether

anyone complained about harassment by
that person?

- Are there any notes, physical evidence,
  or other documentation regarding the
  incident(s)?
- How would you like to see the situation
  resolved?
- Do you know of any other relevant
  information?

Questions to Ask the Alleged Harasser:

- What is your response to the allegations?
- If the harasser claims that the allegations
  are false, ask why the complainant might
  lie.
- Are there any persons who have relevant
  information?
- Are there any notes, physical evidence,
  or other documentation regarding the
  incident(s)?
- Do you know of any other relevant
  information?

Questions to Ask Third Parties:

- What did you see or hear? When did this
  occur? Describe the alleged harasser's
  behavior toward the complainant and
  toward others in the workplace.
- What did the complainant tell you? When
  did s/he tell you this?

- Do you know of any other relevant information?
- Are there other persons who have relevant information?

ii. Credibility Determinations

If there are conflicting versions of relevant events, the employer will have to weigh each party's credibility. Credibility assessments can be critical in determining whether the alleged harassment in fact occurred. Factors to consider include:

- **Inherent plausibility:** Is the testimony believable on its face? Does it make sense?
- **Demeanor:** Did the person seem to be telling the truth or lying?
- **Motive to falsify:** Did the person have a reason to lie?
- **Corroboration:** Is there witness testimony (such as testimony by eye-witnesses, people who saw the person soon after the alleged incidents, or people who discussed the incidents with him or her at around the time that they occurred) or **physical evidence** (such as written documentation) that corroborates the party's testimony?
- **Past record:** Did the alleged harasser have a history of similar behavior in the past?

None of the above factors are determinative as to credibility. For example, the fact that there are no eye-witnesses to the alleged harassment by no means necessarily defeats the complainant's credibility, since harassment often occurs behind closed doors. Furthermore, the fact that the alleged harasser engaged in similar behavior in the past does not necessarily mean that he or she did so again.

iii. Reaching a Determination

Once all of the evidence is in, interviews are finalized, and credibility issues are resolved, management should make a determination as to whether harassment occurred. That determination could be made by the investigator, or by a management official who reviews the investigator's report. The parties should be informed of the determination.

In some circumstances, it may be difficult for management to reach a determination because of direct contradictions between the parties and a lack of documentary or eye-witness corroboration. In such cases, a credibility assessment may form the basis for a determination, based on factors such as those set forth above.

If no determination can be made because the evidence is inconclusive, the employer should still undertake further preventive measures, such as training and monitoring.

f. Assurance of Immediate and Appropriate Corrective Action

An employer should make clear that it will undertake immediate and appropriate corrective action, including discipline, whenever it determines that harassment has occurred in violation of the employer's policy. Management should inform both parties about these measures.[69]

Remedial measures should be designed to stop the harassment, correct its effects on the employee, and ensure that the harassment does not recur. These remedial measures need not be those that the employee requests or prefers, as long as they are effective.

In determining disciplinary measures, management should keep in mind that the employer could be found liable if the harassment does not stop. At the same time, management may have concerns that overly punitive measures may subject the employer

---

[69] Management may be reluctant to release information about specific disciplinary measures that it undertakes against the harasser, due to concerns about potential defamation claims by the harasser. However, many courts have recognized that limited disclosures of such information are privileged. For cases addressing defenses to defamation claims arising out of alleged harassment, *see Duffy v. Leading Edge Products*, 44 F.3d 308, 311 (5th Cir. 1995) (qualified privilege applied to statements accusing plaintiff of harassment); *Garziano v. E.I. DuPont de Nemours & Co.*, 818 F.2d 380 (5th Cir. 1987) (qualified privilege protects employer's statements in bulletin to employees concerning dismissal of alleged harasser): *Stockley v. AT&T*, 687 F. Supp. 764 (E.D.N.Y. 1988) (statements made in course of investigation into sexual harassment charges protected by qualified privilege).

to claims such as wrongful discharge and may simply be inappropriate.

To balance the competing concerns, disciplinary measures should be proportional to the seriousness of the offense.[70] If the harassment was minor, such as a small number of "off-color" remarks by an individual with no prior history of similar misconduct, then counseling and an oral warning might be all that is necessary. On the other hand, if the harassment was severe or persistent, then suspension or discharge may be appropriate.[71]

Remedial measures should not adversely affect the complainant. Thus, for example, if it is necessary to separate the parties, then the harasser should be transferred (unless the complainant prefers

---

[70] *Mockler v. Multnomah County*, 140 F.3d 808, 813 (9th Cir. 1998).

[71] In some cases, accused harassers who were subjected to discipline and subsequently exonerated have claimed that the disciplinary action was discriminatory. No discrimination will be found if the employer had a good faith belief that such action was warranted and there is no evidence that it undertook less punitive measures against similarly situated employees outside his or her protected class who were accused of harassment. In such circumstances, the Commission will not find pretext based solely on an after-the-fact conclusion that the disciplinary action was inappropriate. *See Waggoner v. City of Garland Tex.*, 987 F.2d 1160, 1165 (5th Cir. 1993) (where accused harasser claims that disciplinary action was discriminatory, "[t]he real issue is whether the employer reasonably believed the employee's allegation [of harassment] and acted on it in good faith, or to the contrary, the employer did not actually believe the co-employee's allegation but instead used it as a pretext for an otherwise discriminatory dismissal").

otherwise).[72] Remedial responses that penalize the complainant could constitute unlawful retaliation and are not effective in correcting the harassment.[73]

Remedial measures also should correct the effects of the harassment. Such measures should be designed to put the employee in the position s/he would have been in had the misconduct not occurred.

Examples of Measures to Stop the Harassment and Ensure that it Does Not Recur:

- oral[74] or written warning or reprimand;
- transfer or reassignment;
- demotion;
- reduction of wages;
- suspension;
- discharge;
- training or counseling of harasser to ensure that s/he understands why his or her conduct

---

[72] *See Steiner v. Showboat Operating Co.,* 25 F.3d 1459, 1464 (9th Cir. 1994) (employer remedial action for sexual harassment by supervisor inadequate where it twice changed plaintiff's shift to get her away from supervisor rather than change his shift or work area), *cert. denied,* 513 U.S. 1082 (1995).

[73] *See Guess v. Bethlehem Steel Corp.,* 913 F.2d 463, 465 (7th Cir. 1990) ("a remedial measure that makes the victim of sexual harassment worse off is ineffective *per se*").

[74] An oral warning or reprimand would be appropriate only if the misconduct was isolated and minor. If an employer relies on oral warnings or reprimands to correct harassment, it will have difficulty proving that it exercised reasonable care to prevent and correct such misconduct.

violated the employer's anti-harassment policy; and

- monitoring of harasser to ensure that harassment stops.

Examples of Measures to Correct the Effects of the Harassment:

- restoration of leave taken because of the harassment;
- expungement of negative evaluation(s) in employee's personnel file that arose from the harassment;
- reinstatement;
- apology by the harasser;
- monitoring treatment of employee to ensure that s/he is not subjected to retaliation by the harasser or others in the work place because of the complaint; and
- correction of any other harm caused by the harassment (*e.g.*, compensation for losses).

2. Other Preventive and Corrective Measures

An employer's responsibility to exercise reasonable care to prevent and correct harassment is not limited to implementing an anti-harassment policy and complaint procedure. As the Supreme Court stated, "the employer has a greater opportunity to guard against misconduct by supervisors than by common workers; employers have greater opportunity and incentive to screen them, train them, and monitor their performance." *Faragher,* 118 S. Ct. at 2291.

An employer's duty to exercise due care includes instructing all of its supervisors and managers to address or report to appropriate officials complaints of harassment regardless of whether they are officially designated to take complaints[75] and regardless of whether a complaint was framed in a way that conforms to the organization's particular complaint procedures.[76] For example, if an employee files an EEOC charge alleging unlawful harassment, the employer should launch an internal investigation even if the employee did not complain to management through its internal complaint process.

Furthermore, due care requires management to correct harassment regardless of whether an employee files an internal complaint, if the conduct is clearly unwelcome. For example, if there are areas in the workplace

---

[75] *See Varner,* 94 F.3d at 1213 (complaint procedure is not effective if it does not require supervisor with knowledge of harassment to report the information to those in position to take appropriate action), *cert. denied,*117 S. Ct. 946 (1997); *accord Wilson v. Tulsa Junior College,* 164 F.3d at 541.

[76] *See Wilson,* 164 F.3d at 541 (complaint procedure deficient because it only required supervisors to report "formal" as opposed to "informal" complaints of harassment).

with graffiti containing racial or sexual epithets, management should eliminate the graffiti and not wait for an internal complaint.[77]

An employer should ensure that its supervisors and managers understand their responsibilities under the organization's anti-harassment policy and complaint procedure. Periodic training of those individuals can help achieve that result. Such training should explain the types of conduct that violate the employer's anti-harassment policy; the seriousness of the policy; the responsibilities of supervisors and managers when they learn of alleged harassment; and the prohibition against retaliation.

An employer should keep track of its supervisors' and managers' conduct to make sure that they carry out their responsibilities under the organization's anti-harassment program.[78] For example, an employer could include such compliance in formal evaluations.

---

[77] See, e.g., Splunge v. Shoney's, Inc., 97 F.3d 488, 490 (11th Cir. 1996) (where harassment of plaintiffs was so pervasive that higher management could be deemed to have constructive knowledge of it, employer was obliged to undertake corrective action even though plaintiff did not register complaints); Fall v. Indiana Univ. Bd. Of Trustees, 12 F. Supp.2d 870, 882 (N.D. Ind. 1998) (employer has constructive knowledge of harassment by supervisors where it "was so broad in scope and so permeated the workplace that it must have come to the attention of someone authorized to do something about it").

[78] In Faragher, the City lost the opportunity to establish the affirmative defense in part because "its officials made no attempt to keep track of the conduct of supervisors." Faragher, 118 S. Ct. at 2293.

Reasonable preventive measures include screening applicants for supervisory jobs to see if any have a record of engaging in harassment. If so, it may be necessary for the employer to reject a candidate on that basis or to take additional steps to prevent harassment by that individual.

Finally, it is advisable for an employer to keep records of all complaints of harassment. Without such records, the employer could be unaware of a pattern of harassment by the same individual. Such a pattern would be relevant to credibility assessments and disciplinary measures.[79]

3. Small Businesses

It may not be necessary for an employer of a small workforce to implement the type of formal complaint process described above. If it puts into place an effective, informal mechanism to prevent and correct harassment, a small employer could still satisfy the first prong of the affirmative defense to a claim of harassment.[80] As the Court recognized in *Faragher*, an employer of a small workforce might informally exercise sufficient care to prevent harassment.[81]

---

[79] See Subsections V(C)(1)(e)(ii) and V(C)(2), above.

[80] If the owner of the business commits unlawful harassment, then the business will automatically be found liable under the alter ego standard and no affirmative defense can be raised. *See* Section VI, below.

[81] *Faragher*, 118 S. Ct. at 2293.

For example, such an employer's failure to disseminate a written policy against harassment on protected
bases would not undermine the affirmative defense
if it effectively communicated the prohibition and an
effective complaint procedure to all employees at staff
meetings. An owner of a small business who regularly
meets with all of his or her employees might tell them
at monthly staff meetings that he or she will not tolerate
harassment and that anyone who experiences harassment should bring it "straight to the top."

If a complaint is made, the business, like any other
employer, must conduct a prompt, thorough, and impartial investigation and undertake swift and appropriate
corrective action where appropriate. The questions set
forth in Section V(C)(1)(e)(i), above, can help guide the
inquiry and the factors set forth in Section V(C)(1)(e)(ii)
should be considered in evaluating the credibility of
each of the parties.

D. Second Prong of Affirmative Defense: Employee's Duty to Exercise Reasonable Care

The second prong of the affirmative defense requires
a showing by the employer that the aggrieved employee
"unreasonably failed to take advantage of any preventive
or corrective opportunities provided by the employer or to
avoid harm otherwise." *Faragher,* 118 S. Ct. at 2293; *Ellerth,*
118 S. Ct. at 2270.

This element of the defense arises from the general theory
"that a victim has a duty 'to use such means as are reasonable

under the circumstances to avoid or minimize the damages' that result from violations of the statute." *Faragher,* 18 S. Ct. at 2292, *quoting Ford Motor Co. v. EEOC,* 458 U.S. 219, 231 n.15 (1982). Thus an employer who exercised reasonable care as described in subsection V(C), above, is not liable for unlawful harassment if the aggrieved employee could have avoided all of the actionable harm. If some but not all of the harm could have been avoided, then an award of damages will be mitigated accordingly.[82]

A complaint by an employee does not automatically defeat the employer's affirmative defense. If, for example, the employee provided no information to support his or her allegation, gave untruthful information, or otherwise failed to cooperate in the investigation, the complaint would not qualify as an effort to avoid harm. Furthermore, if the employee unreasonably delayed complaining, and an earlier complaint could have reduced the harm, then the affirmative defense could operate to reduce damages.

Proof that the employee unreasonably failed to use any complaint procedure provided by the employer will normally satisfy the employer's burden.[83] However, it is important to

---

[82] *Faragher,* 118 S. Ct. at 2292 ("If the victim could have avoided harm, no liability should be found against the employer who had taken reasonable care, and if damages could reasonably have been mitigated no award against liable employer should reward a plaintiff for what her own efforts could have avoided.").

[83] *Ellerth,* 118 S. Ct. at 2270; *Faragher,* 118 S. Ct. at 2293. *See also Scrivner v. Socorro Independent School District,* 169 F.3d 969, 971 (5th Cir. 1999) (employer established second prong of defense where harassment began during summer, plaintiff misled investigators inquiring into anonymous complaint by denying that harassment occurred, and plaintiff did not complain about the harassment until the following March).

emphasize that an employee who failed to complain does not carry a burden of proving the reasonableness of that decision. Rather, the burden lies with the employer to prove that the employee's failure to complain was unreasonable.

1. Failure to Complain

A determination as to whether an employee unreasonably failed to complain or otherwise avoid harm depends on the particular circumstances and information available to the employee *at that time.*[84] An employee should not necessarily be expected to complain to management immediately after the first or second incident of relatively minor harassment. Workplaces need not become battlegrounds where every minor, unwelcome remark based on race, sex, or another protected category triggers a complaint and investigation. An employee might reasonably ignore a small number of incidents, hoping that the harassment will stop without resort to the complaint process.[85] The employee may directly say to the harasser that s/he wants the misconduct to stop, and then wait to see if that is effective in ending the harassment before complaining to management. If the harassment persists, however, then further delay in complaining might be found unreasonable.

---

[84] The employee is not required to have chosen "the course that events later show to have been the best." Restatement (Second) of Torts § 918, comment c.

[85] *See Corcoran v. Shoney's Colonial, Inc.,* 24 F. Supp.2d 601, 606 (W.D. Va. 1998) ("Though unwanted sexual remarks have no place in the work environment, it is far uncommon for those subjected to such remarks to ignore them when they are first made.").

There might be other reasonable explanations for an employee's delay in complaining or entire failure to utilize the employer's complaint process. For example, the employee might have had reason to believe that:[86]

- using the complaint mechanism entailed a risk of retaliation;
- there were obstacles to complaints; and
- the complaint mechanism was not effective.

To establish the second prong of the affirmative defense, the employer must prove that the belief or perception underlying the employee's failure to complain was unreasonable.

a. Risk of Retaliation

An employer cannot establish that an employee unreasonably failed to use its complaint procedure if that employee reasonably feared retaliation. Surveys have shown that employees who are subjected to harassment frequently do not complain to management due to fear of retaliation.[87] To assure employees that such a fear is unwarranted, the employer must

---

[86] *See Faragher,* 118 S. Ct. at 2292 (defense established if plaintiff unreasonably failed to avail herself of "a proven, effective mechanism for reporting and resolving complaints of sexual harassment, available to the employee without undue risk or expense"). *See also* Restatement (Second) of Torts § 918, comment c (tort victim "is not barred from full recovery by the fact that it would have been reasonable for him to make expenditures or subject himself to pain or risk; it is only when he is unreasonable in refusing or failing to take action to prevent further loss that his damages are curtailed").

[87] *See* n.59, above.

clearly communicate and enforce a policy that no employee will be retaliated against for complaining of harassment.

b. Obstacles to Complaints

An employee's failure to use the employer's complaint procedure would be reasonable if that failure was based on unnecessary obstacles to complaints. For example, if the process entailed undue expense by the employee,[88] inaccessible points of contact for making complaints,[89] or unnecessarily intimidating or burdensome requirements, failure to invoke it on such a basis would be reasonable.

An employee's failure to participate in a mandatory mediation or other alternative dispute resolution process also does not constitute unreasonable failure to avoid harm. While an employee can be expected to cooperate in the employer's investigation by providing relevant information, an employee can never be required to waive rights, either substantive or procedural, as an element of his or her exercise of reasonable care.[90] Nor must an

---

[88] See Faragher, 118 S. Ct. at 2292 (employee should not recover for harm that could have been avoided by utilizing a proven, effective complaint process that was available "without undue risk or expense").

[89] See Wilson, 164 F.3d at 541 (complaint process deficient where official who could take complaint was inaccessible due to hours of duty and location in separate facility).

[90] See Policy Statement on Mandatory Binding Arbitration of Employment Discrimination Disputes as a Condition of Employment, EEOC Compliance Manual (BNA) N:3101 (7/10/97).

employee have to try to resolve the matter with the harasser as an element of exercising due care.

c. Perception That Complaint Process Was Ineffective

An employer cannot establish the second prong of the defense based on the employee's failure to complain if that failure was based on a reasonable belief that the process was ineffective. For example, an employee would have a reasonable basis to believe that the complaint process is ineffective if the procedure required the employee to complain initially to the harassing supervisor. Such a reasonable basis also would be found if he or she was aware of instances in which coworkers' complaints failed to stop harassment. One way to increase employees' confidence in the efficacy of the complaint process would be for the employer to release general information to employees about corrective and disciplinary measures undertaken to stop harassment.[91]

2. Other Efforts to Avoid Harm

Generally, an employer can prove the second prong of the affirmative defense if the employee unreasonably failed to utilize its complaint process. However, such proof will not establish the defense if the employee made other efforts to avoid harm.

---

[91] For a discussion of defamation claims and the application of a qualified privilege to an employer's statements about instances of harassment, *see* n.69, above.

For example, a prompt complaint by the employee to the EEOC or a state fair employment practices agency while the harassment is ongoing could qualify as such an effort. A union grievance could also qualify as an effort to avoid harm.[92] Similarly, a staffing firm worker who is harassed at the client's workplace might report the harassment either to the staffing firm or to the client, reasonably expecting that either would act to correct the problem.[93] Thus the worker's failure to complain to one of those entities would not bar him or her from subsequently bringing a claim against it.

With these and any other efforts to avoid harm, the timing of the complaint could affect liability or damages. If the employee could have avoided some of the harm by complaining earlier, then damages would be mitigated accordingly.

VI. Harassment by "Alter Ego" of Employer
A. *Standard of Liability*

An employer is liable for unlawful harassment whenever the harasser is of a sufficiently high rank to fall "within

---

[92] *See Watts v. Kroger Company,* 170 F.3d 505, 510 (5th Cir. 1999) (plaintiff made effort "to avoid harm otherwise" where she filed a union grievance and did not utilize the employer's harassment complaint process; both the employer and union procedures were corrective mechanisms designed to avoid harm).

[93] Both the staffing firm and the client may be legally responsible, under the anti-discrimination statutes, for undertaking correction action. *See* Enforcement Guidance: Application of EEO Laws to Contingent Workers Placed by Temporary Employment Agencies and Other Staffing Firms, EEOC Compliance Manual (BNA) N:3317 (12/3/97).

that class...who may be treated as the organization's proxy." *Faragher*, 118 S. Ct. at 2284.[94] In such circumstances, the official's unlawful harassment is imputed automatically to the employer.[95] Thus the employer cannot raise the affirmative defense, even if the harassment did not result in a tangible employment action.

B. Officials Who Qualify as "Alter Egos" or "Proxies"

The Court, in *Faragher*, cited the following examples of officials whose harassment could be imputed automatically to the employer:

- president[96]
- owner[97]
- partner[98]
- corporate officer

---

[94] *See also Ellerth*, 118 S. Ct. at 2267 (under agency principles an employer is indirectly liable "where the agent's high rank in the company makes him or her the employer's alter ago"); *Harrison v. Eddy Potash, Inc.*, 158 F.3d 1371, 1376 (10th Cir. 1998) ("the Supreme Court in Burlington acknowledged an employer can be held vicariously liable under Title VII if the harassing employer's 'high rank in the company makes him or her the employer's alter ego'").

[95] *Faragher*, 118 S. Ct. at 2284.

[96] The Court noted that the standards for employer liability were not at issue in the case of *Harris v. Forklift Systems*, 510 U.S. 17 (1993), because the harasser was the president of the company. *Faragher*, 118 S. Ct. at 2284.

[97] An individual who has an ownership interest in an organization, receives compensation based on its profits, and participates in managing the organization would qualify as an "owner" or "partner." *Serapion v. Martinez*, 119 F.3d 982, 990 (1st Cir. 1997), *cert. denied*, 118 S. Ct. 690 (1998).

[98] *Id.*

VII. Conclusion

The Supreme Court's rulings in *Ellerth* and *Faragher* create an incentive for employers to implement and enforce strong policies prohibiting harassment and effective complaint procedures. The rulings also create an incentive for employees to alert management about harassment before it becomes severe and pervasive. If employers and employees undertake these steps, unlawful harassment can often be prevented, thereby effectuating an important goal of the anti-discrimination statutes.

Glossary of Terms

ADR Alternative Dispute Resolution—resolutions that fall outside traditional judicial methods

CLE Continuing Legal Education—required training for attorneys to retain their right to practice law after passing the bar

Consumer Report—written or oral communications from a consumer reporting agency which bear upon an individual's character, credit worthiness, general reputation, personal characteristics or mode of living

EEOC Equal Employment Opportunity Commission—The agency of the United States Government that enforces federal employment discrimination laws

EPLI Employment Practices Liability Insurance

Ellerth/Faragher Defense—defense in which employers may avoid certain liability for claims of hostile work environment harassment committed by supervisors and employees

FACT Act Fair and Accurate Credit Transactions Act—sections added to the Fair Credit Reporting Act, intended to help consumers protect themselves from identity theft

FCRA Fair Credit Reporting Act—law that regulates collection, dissemination, and use of consumer credit information

FTC Federal Trade Commission—division of the federal government in charge of anticompetitive and consumer protection laws

FLSA Fair Labor Standards Act—sets requirements for minimum wage, overtime pay, recordkeeping, and child labor

Investigative Consumer Report—written or oral communications from a consumer reporting agency and information gathered from interviews that bear upon an individual's character, credit worthiness, general reputation, personal characteristics or mode of living

NLRA National Labor Relations Act—contains guidelines for employers with regards to labor organizations

OWBPA Older Workers' Benefits Protection Act—prohibits employers from denying benefits to older employees

OHSA Occupational Safety and Health Administration—federal department that ensures safe and healthy work environments

SEC Securities and Exchange Commission—division of government that protects investors and regulates markets

Vail Letter—letter in which the FTC suggested that notice and disclosure rules of the FCRA must be followed when investigating misconduct claims

Index

discharge
    accounting for possibility
      of, 42
    company policy regarding,
      28–9
    FACT Act and, 63
discipline, company policy
    regarding, 28–9
    EEOC guidance for, 120–6
disruption to business
    accounting for, 42
    reducing, 23–4, 34–5, 42
documentary evidence,
    gathering, 52–3

Ellerth/Faragher defense, 19–20
    glossary entry for, 137
    Also see Appendix.
email, company policy regarding,
    31, 53
employee files, viewing, 72–3
employment practices liability
    insurance (EPLI), 10–11, 32
Equal Employment Opportunity
    (EEO) laws
    company policy regarding,
      28–9
    Also see Appendix.
Equal Employment Opportunity
    Commission (EEOC)
    glossary entry for, 137
    guidelines for
      investigations, 24, 68–9
    Also see Appendix.
ethics, company policy regarding,
    29
evidence
    confirming, 54
    documenting, 52–3
    gathering, 40, 41, 52–3
    preserving, 54

Fair and Accurate Credit
    Transitions (FACT) Act
    glossary entry for, 138
    requirements of, 59–63
    summary of, 61–3
Fair Credit Reporting Act (FCRA)
    glossary entry for, 138
    requirements of, 59–60
Fair Labor Standards Act
    (FLSA), 138
fairness, perceived, 19, 241
Farager v. City of Boca Raton, 19
Federal Trade Commission (FTC)
    glossary entry for, 138
    interpretation of FCRA of,
      59–60
feedback to involved parties,
    providing, 58
files, investigation, 70
findings, investigation, 54–5
follow-up to investigations, 57

gender differences, cultural, 45–6

harassment
    company policy regarding,
      28–9, 30, 46, 108–9
    vicarious liability for
      harrassment by
      supervisors. *See
      Appendix.*
human resource professionals
    expertise of, 6–8, 17
    as investigators, 15–19, 22–3,
      66, 70–1, 73, 75–6
    outside counsel and, 2–4

inconclusive findings, 55–6
industry knowledge, counsel's,
    6, 8
initial complaints, handling, 37–9

searches, workplace, 52–3

Securities and Exchange
   Commission (SEC)
      glossary entry for, 138
      requirements, 69

self-regulatory organizations,
   FACT Act and, 62

small legal firms, using, 8–9

summary reports
      of interviews, 66
      reliability of, 70–1

technology, company policy
   regarding, 31

termination. *See* discharge.

third-party investigators, benefits
   of using, 18–23

timeline of events, preparing, 44,
   53–4, 55–6

transcripts, interview, 47–8, 54,
   65–6

uncooperative witnesses,
   handling, 72

unionized workplaces, 2, 42

Vail Letters
      glossary entry for, 138
      requirements of, 59–60, 138

vicarious employer liability. *See
Appendix.*

violence, company policy
   regarding, 30

workplace searches, company
   policy regarding, 30

www.ingramcontent.com/pod-product-compliance
Lightning Source LLC
Chambersburg PA
CBHW020706270326
41928CB00005B/289